THE TRINITY,
Practically Speaking

THE TRINITY,
Practically Speaking

FRANK D. MACCHIA

Biblica Publishing
We welcome your questions and comments.

USA   1820 Jet Stream Drive, Colorado Springs, CO 80921
        www.Biblica.com

The Trinity, Practically Speaking
ISBN-13: 978-1-60657-008-1

12 11 10 / 6 5 4 3 2 1

Published in 2010 by Biblica Publishing

A catalog record for this book is available through the Library of Congress.

Printed in the United States of America

For Desiree and Jasmine —
That they will flourish within the embrace of the triune God.

CONTENTS

ACKNOWLEDGEMENTS

I want to thank my wife, Verena, and my daughters, Jasmine and Desiree, for their patience as I put my many thoughts on paper towards the completion of this manuscript. The dedication to my daughters is but a small token of this gratitude. Gratitude also belongs to Gilbert Chen for reading chapters and for offering helpful suggestions on how I might communicate my ideas more effectively. Lastly, thanks to all of my family and friends, especially at Grace Bible Church in Irvine, California, for encouraging me to write something that is accessible to a general audience. Blessings on them all.

CONCERNING A PRACTICAL NECESSITY

My nephew Anthony looked at me and said, "Explain the doctrine of the Trinity to me!" He was only twelve years old. How was I to do this? I tried to use one example after another, but he seemed unsatisfied. Many of us have had this experience. We learn very quickly that even basic biblical truths can be difficult to understand and explain. And yet, the doctrine of the Trinity is a practical necessity to the Christian life. We simply cannot do without it. This is because there is a basic logic to Scripture and to Christian faith when it comes to how we speak about God that necessitates the doctrine of the Trinity. I will attempt to explain the practical necessity of the Trinity as a doctrine in the pages that follow.

Suffice it to say here that this doctrine is needed for us to talk about God in a way that avoids serious error. Not many people, however, have viewed the idea of the Trinity as having much practical value. In fact, it has puzzled many. The idea that the one God is eternally three persons (Father, Son, and Holy Spirit) has appeared more as an intellectual puzzle than a practical necessity. How can God be one and three at the same time? Even sincere Christians have wondered whether this conception is really biblical or actually necessary to the Christian life.

Yet I am convinced that the doctrine of the Trinity is necessitated by the assumptions and practices of the Christian faith, whether we know it or not. There is a certain logic implied in the Scriptures and in the practical life of faith that leads inescapably to the doctrine of the Trinity. In fact, it is implied in our faith in Christ as our Redeemer and in our worship of him as Lord. It is implied in our adoration of the Holy Spirit as God's presence among us and in our assumption that God is a circle of love into which we come for fellowship.

Our awareness that the truth of the Trinity is demanded by the Scriptures and the practical life of faith can profoundly expand our understanding of the richness of the Christian life. So, I have thought for quite some time that a book needs to be written that convinces the people of God of the practical necessity and value of the doctrine of the Trinity. Though the reasoning of faith that leads to this truth is important, it begins, proceeds, and ends in God's loving embrace and in our adoration of God within this embrace. I pray that the following study will bless the reader with greater insight into that divine love that passes all understanding, the love shared among Father, Son, and Holy Spirit.

1
OUR TRAIN TO WEST BERLIN
The Logic of Faith

Logic begins with a basic premise and then proceeds to a conclusion. For example, if my premise is that *only* a college graduate can get a job that pays well, I would then have to conclude that everyone with a job that pays well is a college graduate. It would not take very long to realize, however, that this premise is not valid, making the conclusion also invalid. But if a premise is valid, then the conclusion drawn from it is valid as well. For example, if my premise is that God loves all human beings, and I am a human being, then it follows of logical necessity that God loves *me*. Moving through a reasoning process can be compared to taking a journey by train and passing through various stations. I will explain this comparison more precisely as we proceed.

This introductory chapter is about the inherent logic of Scripture when it comes to the crucial issue of God's identity. Who is God? The average person might immediately respond that "God is God! There is simply no more to say than that!" This is an understandable response, but surely such an answer is not satisfying. So we would be justified in asking again, "Who *is* God?" If pressed further, someone might answer that God is loving or gracious or sovereign. But these are characteristics or attributes of God. It would be like saying that my father is kind or strict. If someone were to ask, "Who *is* your father?" I would want to say something more than what he is like. I would want to identify him by his name.

So when we say what God is like (loving or sovereign), we still have not said anything directly about God's *identity*. The biblical answer to God's identity is complex and multifaceted. For example, God is named the great "I AM WHO I AM" (or "WILL BE") in Exodus 3:14, from which we get the name *Yahweh* or *Jehovah*. God said to Israel that he "is" (or "will be") what he has promised to be as Israel's liberator from bondage, especially in the exodus from Egypt (see Exodus 6:2–8). That God "always is" who God is ("I am who I am") as Savior witnesses to God's unchanging faithfulness.

God's name is future oriented (God always will be what God is), because it is tied to a divine pledge to fulfill a promise to be the Liberator and Savior in the exodus and beyond. The future of this promise is ultimately fulfilled in Jesus Christ, for there is now no other name by which we are saved but his (Acts 4:12). The name *Jesus* refers to God's role as Savior: "You are to give him the name Jesus, because he will save his people from their sins" (Matthew 1:21). So the name of God is now tied decisively to the story of Jesus, where the great "I Am" (or "Will Be") is decisively revealed (Hebrews 1:1–3). God is revealed in the story of Jesus not only as the Son, Jesus Christ, but also as his heavenly Father and as the Holy Spirit who comes from the Father to rest on Jesus. But then the Spirit that is poured out through Jesus fulfills God's saving identity in the context of a promise of a future new creation. God is ultimately identified here as "Father, Son, and Holy Spirit." This is at the base of what it means to say that God is a trinity. But there is more to say. We need to show that God is indeed named as a trinity in the Scripture before we can probe the necessary logic (premise and conclusion) that necessitates this doctrine.

Is God Really Named as a Trinity in Scripture?

I was in the middle of a lecture on the Trinity at the university where I teach when a young woman with a look of concern on her face raised her hand as though she had something urgent to say. I was in the process of explaining that the doctrine of the Trinity is one of the most important doctrines of the Christian church, since it summarizes so well other key doctrines, such as salvation by grace and the deity of Christ. I thought that I was gaining momentum, about ready to bring home an important point, when her hand went up. Upon my calling on her, she immediately protested that the term *Trinity* is not found in the Bible. "Yes, I know," I responded, and then tried to explain to her that the concept is biblical nonetheless.

Not satisfied, she pressed on, "But aren't you using a term from outside of the Bible to distract attention away from the simple gospel, causing a lot of needless confusion?" I then asked her if John 3:16 would qualify as a statement of the simple gospel: "For God so loved the world that he gave his one and only Son, that whoever believes in him shall not perish but have eternal life." I could tell by her nod that she did. I then noted that according to this text the Son was sent into the world by his heavenly Father in order to impart the eternal life given in the gift of the Holy Spirit. "So it seems that the simple gospel is about the cooperative work of the Father, the Son, and the Holy Spirit," I added. "That sounds like a fairly good description of the Trinity to me." I could see a smile begin to form on her face, as though it were making sense to her.

Indeed, the simple gospel is a story that involves not only Jesus but actually *three* major players: the heavenly Father, Jesus as the one and only Son of the Father, and the Holy Spirit who comes forth from the Father and is given to us through Jesus so that we might have new life. So who are these three players? If the good news of Jesus Christ celebrates a salvation that they provide for us, I think it is extremely important to discover who they are. This is precisely what the doctrine of the Trinity attempts to do—to identify them for us.

The term *Trinity* is not in the Bible, but the meaning of the term is there throughout the New Testament and is inescapable in any summary of the simple gospel of Jesus Christ. It is not the term that is important but rather what it points to. The fact of the Trinity usually seems apparent to anyone who has read the New Testament or gone to church for any length of time. After all, we cannot read the New Testament without coming across numerous references to the heavenly Father or to the Son of God, Jesus Christ, or to the Holy Spirit. We cannot pray, worship, or witness without naming God in this way. We pray to the heavenly Father, through the Son, and in the power of the Holy Spirit. Or, we pray to the Son, Jesus Christ, in the power of the Holy Spirit and to the glory of the Father. Either way, prayer compels us to name God as Father, Son, and Holy Spirit.

The reason we are so compelled to name God in this way is because God has willed to be named this way. This naming is authentic, because it is how God is self-revealed. It is faithful to who God is eternally. God is revealed in the story of Jesus as the heavenly Father of Jesus Christ and as Jesus, the one and only Son of the Father, and as the Holy Spirit sent forth from the Father through the Son into the world. Acts 2:33 notes concerning Jesus after his ascension to heaven, "Exalted to the right hand of God, he has received from the Father the promised Holy Spirit and has poured out what you now see and hear." After the resurrection, the Son ascended to the right hand of the heavenly Father in order to receive the Holy Spirit and to pour forth the Spirit on us. God is named in the story of Jesus as the Father, the Son, and the Holy Spirit.

Actually, every event in the story of Jesus identifies God in this way, as Father, Son, and Holy Spirit. All three are present and accounted for, cooperating and interacting, in every event of Jesus' life. Jesus was the Son sent from the Father and conceived in Mary's womb by the power of the Holy Spirit (Luke 1:35). Later, at his baptism, Jesus heard the voice of the Father speaking, "You are my Son, whom I love; with you I am well pleased," and at this moment, the Holy Spirit was seen descending on him (Luke 3:22). At his crucifixion, Jesus offered up his life to the Father by "the eternal Spirit" (Hebrews 9:14), as the Father offered up the Son out of love for the world (Romans 8:32). At the resurrection, the Father vindicated the condemned and crucified Jesus as the favored Son by raising Jesus from the dead according to "the Spirit of holiness" (Romans 1:4). Jesus then ascended to the right hand of the Father in order to receive the Holy Spirit once more and then to pour forth the Spirit on the disciples (Acts 2:33), much like the Father had poured forth the Spirit on Jesus earlier at his baptism.

So God is defined in every event of Jesus' life as the Father, the Son, and the Holy Spirit. Loyal to the story of Jesus, the New Testament speaks of God throughout as Father, Son, and Holy Spirit (Romans 15:30; 1 Corinthians 12:4–6; 2 Corinthians 13:14; Ephesians 1:17, 4:4–6; 1 Peter 1:2). When asked who God is, someone faithful to the Scriptures and to the life of the church will simply have to answer, "Father, Son, and Holy Spirit." This is what we call the divine *Trinity*. This is who God is.

Someone might say at this point, "Hold on! Not so fast! Though the New Testament speaks a lot about the Father, the Son, and the Holy Spirit, how do we know that *all three* are being defined as God? After all, doesn't the Bible clearly state that there is only one

God? Deuteronomy 6:4 says, 'Hear, O Israel: The LORD our God, the LORD is one.' How can we now say that according to the New Testament, God is three?" Traditionally, the church has answered this question by noting that God is *one* in one way and *three* in another. God is one as to God's very being (or nature) and is three as to persons.

Let's explore this a little. We know that God is one. There is no possibility that there are three separate gods. Speaking in the first person singular ("I"), God said, "I am the LORD, and there is no other; apart from me there is no God" (Isaiah 45:5). God spoke as a singular "I" (and not a "we"), and clearly said that there is no other God. There is no possibility for divided loyalty when it comes to faith in God, for there is only one God, one Lord, who commands our allegiance (see Deuteronomy 6:4–5). The biblical assumption concerning God is that only the God (singular) of creation or of the exodus (or, later, of Jesus Christ) can save. There are no other divine beings to appeal to. There are no other possibilities.

But we also know that God is three distinct persons. This three-ness of person in God is shown in the interaction that takes place within God, in the fact that the Father, the Son, and the Holy Spirit personally interact in Scripture, an interaction that has existed for eternity. Note the first person plural in Genesis 1:26, as God said, "Let us make human beings in our image" (TNIV, which may be viewed as a conversation internal to God rather than externally with us). The Son and the Father have loved each other throughout all eternity and shared the glory of deity with each other even before the worlds were made (John 17:5, 24). The Son said to the heavenly Father, "You sent me into the world" (John 17:18), meaning that the Son was sent by the Father into the world—obviously referring to the divine Word's becoming flesh (John 1:14) or to the Son who was at the Father's side and who came into flesh to make the Father known (John 1:18). The action of the Son's entering the world involved the Father and the Son long before the Son was conceived in Mary's womb as the baby Jesus. As the Son was coming into the world, he said to the Father, "Sacrifice and offering you did not desire, but a body you prepared for me; with burnt offerings and sin offerings you were not pleased. . . . Here I am—it is written about me in the scroll—I have come to do your will, O God" (Hebrews 10:5–7).

The Son is even said to have been the agent in the Father's act of creating all things (John 1:1–3; Colossians 1:15; Hebrews 1:3). Similarly, the Holy Spirit was there at the creation, too, active with the Father and the Son in creating the world (Genesis 1:2). The Spirit was also there active in the sending of Jesus into the world to be conceived by the virgin Mary (Luke 1:35). The Spirit rested on Jesus and sent him out into the wilderness to be tempted (Mark 1:12). The Holy Spirit interacts with the heavenly Father, as well (Romans 8:26), and will testify about Jesus, according to John 15:26. Clearly, Father, Son, and Holy Spirit interact with each other and love each other and have always done so throughout eternity. Though one being, God is also three distinct persons, inseparable but distinct.

This answer has not satisfied everyone. Some will say that this concept of the eternal God as *three* who is also *one* is still difficult to understand. But consider this: Is the fact that the Trinity is difficult to comprehend a reason for not believing it? Anyone who has gone through a class in physics or calculus will have to admit that something is not false just because it is difficult to understand. After all, we are talking about *God* here, an infinite mind that limitlessly exceeds our minds in greatness and complexity. Is it any wonder that we should find it difficult to understand the identity and existence of such a being? Of course, with the help of God's Spirit we are able to grasp some things about God. But there is also a depth that goes beyond our capacities to fully understand.

Still, some insist that before we can really say that God is Father, Son, and Holy Spirit, there must be a compelling reason for believing it. A difficult concept like this must have strong evidence to support it before we can insist that people accept it. In response to this challenge, the church has typically tried to prove from Scripture that all three persons of God are divine. First, the Father spoken about in the New Testament is God: Ephesians 4:6 refers to "one God and Father of all." Second, Titus 2:13 refers to Jesus as "our great God and Savior." Third, Acts 5:3–5 equates lying to the Holy Spirit with lying to God, implying that the Spirit is also a divine person. (By the way, the personhood of the Spirit is shown here in the fact that it is possible to lie to the Spirit, whereas it is not possible to lie to an impersonal force.) So it seems that all three—Father, Son, and Holy Spirit—are distinct persons of one divine nature, and all three are called God. So far, so good; but even this argument is not sufficient. More must be said in defense of the Trinity.

Some are still not satisfied that God is a trinity. For example, in the fourth century, a church leader named Arius and his followers tried to argue that Jesus and the Holy Spirit are not really divine. Only the heavenly Father is the almighty God. The other two are subordinate to him as lesser beings that were created in time. There are people today who hold a similar view. The church calls them heretics, because they have strayed from truths that are vital to the Christian faith. Such folks will seek to alter the verses mentioned above so as to prove that either Jesus or the Holy Spirit is not divine. For example, they might take Titus 2:13, which speaks of "our great God and Savior, Jesus Christ," and try to make it appear that "God" and "Savior, Jesus Christ" are not both referring to Jesus, but one to God the Father and the other to Jesus the Savior. Is this possible?

No, it is not. Not only is such a reading unjustifiable grammatically, but it contradicts one of the most basic concepts in biblical theology.

I will try to show in this book that the above effort to separate God from the Savior Jesus Christ in Titus 2:13 is theologically impossible. *There is in fact no way that there can be a Savior besides God.* If Jesus is the Savior, he must also be the God referred to there as well. The "great God" and "Savior" in Titus 2:13 must both be references to Jesus. I will explain the inseparable link between God and Savior by using the metaphor of a journey, compelled by the fundamental logic of Scripture. It seems that basing a large concept like the Trinity on a handful of isolated verses is not sufficient. We must probe deeper into the underlying assumptions of Scripture and the conclusions that they demand in order to understand the necessity of belief in the Trinity.

The Logic of Scripture: Making the Journey to the Trinity

When folks travel nowadays they have all of the aids necessary to find their way to their destination without getting lost. We can receive precise directions to any destination from the Internet or by simply entering an address into a global positioning system (GPS) and allowing the robotic voice to guide every turn until a destination is reached. I can still recall, however, when finding precise directions was not so convenient. We had to struggle with large maps and tiny lines and symbols difficult to detect with the naked eye. Our destination was often located just beyond the margin of a map. After locating the appropriate map through difficult maneuvering, we still had to use mental skill and imagination to detect how the destination connected with the point of departure.

Finding our way to God's identity might seem to many today like struggling with maps the old-fashioned way. The Bible is filled with hundreds of pages of narratives, poetry, symbolic prophecies, and letters written by different authors over centuries of time to far-away people in places little known to the average reader. The essential points that these ancient texts make about God may not seem immediately clear to the ordinary reader. I do believe that a dedicated and methodical study of the Bible will reveal many of these points. But I also believe that God has guided the church in this discovery, producing a doctrinal heritage that aids us in detecting the essential points of biblical revelation. Of course, this heritage is no substitute for a direct study of the Scripture that will test and prove every point of the church's shared beliefs. On one level, the purpose of this book is to reveal to the reader the step-by-step path of discovery that led the church through the Scriptures to a discovery of God's identity as the Trinity.

Indeed, the journey to God's identity is not that difficult to navigate once you understand where the biblical map is pointing. As an example, let's talk about mapping steps in logic. The term *logic* turns a lot of Christians off, because they've heard the term used so often against the realities affirmed by faith. "That's not logical!" they may have heard someone say when talking about the reality of God or even of the Trinity. In the history of theology, there is a lengthy tradition that sees faith as directly contrary to reason, including logic. The resurrection of Jesus from the dead seems contrary to logic for many today, but Christians know it to be real, in part because the Spirit that raised Jesus from the dead lives in them.

Yet logic is not to be entirely dismissed. There are premises (foundational ideas or assumptions) that, if true, imply certain consequences. For example, if someone were to say to you, "All human beings are mortal," that would make sense. We know that all people are subject to death and are, therefore, mortal. If someone were then to add that "Socrates is a human being," you would have to conclude then that "Socrates is mortal." Why? The reason is in the premise, namely that *all* human beings are mortal. If *all* human beings are mortal, there is no room for exceptions. If Socrates then can be shown to be a human being, he has to be mortal, too. The premise ("all human beings are mortal") allows for no exceptions.

God gave us minds that think. Why would God not want us to use them in matters of faith? In fact, as we noted at the beginning, an argument can be made that faith implies a certain kind of logic of its own. We could argue that the purpose of theology is to discover the logic of biblical faith and to develop this logic faithfully. This doesn't mean that something is to be rejected just because it doesn't make sense to us according to our current understanding of science or some culturally acquired ideas. Certainly, God is not bound by such humanly acquired assumptions, as valuable as they may be. But the Scriptures do assume certain fundamental principles to which the totality of Scripture remains true.

For example, the Bible says that we are saved by grace and not by our own works (Ephesians 2:8). Though our acts play a secondary role in salvation (by the power of God's grace), salvation is always viewed throughout Scripture fundamentally as a gift of God. We will never find a passage of Scripture that denies this. A number of logical consequences can be taken from this biblical premise that are valuable for preaching and teaching, such as the fact that faith itself is only possible by the power of God's Word (Romans 10:17) and is, therefore, a gift from God (even if we, by God's grace, must still *choose* to believe). So there is logic to scriptural teaching that is valuable to faith, as faith seeks greater wisdom and understanding.

Here's the main point of this book: I believe that a force of logic exists in the Bible concerning God as a trinity. It goes like this:

- Only God can save.
- The Father saves; the Son, Jesus Christ, saves; and the Holy Spirit saves.
- Conclusion: Father, Son, and Holy Spirit are God.

The basic premise given above is that *only God can save*. The Bible from beginning to end is clear on this point, allowing for no exceptions. Hosea 13:4 summarizes it well: "But I am the LORD your God, who brought you out of Egypt. You shall acknowledge no God but me, no Savior except me." There is *no* Savior to be recognized by us *except* the one LORD God of Israel. The phrase "no Savior except me" does not allow for any exceptions or any additional gods; it does not leave any wiggle room to recognize any other saviors. When it comes to salvation, God is the only act in town!

Even God's role as Creator is pictured in Genesis 1 in such a way as to convince the reader that God's breath (Spirit) and Word *alone* bring all things into existence, sustaining and guiding them in their God-willed destinies. The Spirit of God hovered over the face of the deep and God spoke all things into existence (Genesis 1:2–3). The creation has no capacity for life independent of its Creator, which means that the creature has no capacity for new life or salvation apart from God the Creator. The very last book of the Bible agrees, noting that "salvation belongs to our God" (Revelation 7:10). Salvation is a capacity that belongs only to God. This insight forms the basis of the Bible's central conviction that the creature does not have any ability apart from God to free itself from sin or to restore itself to life. Only God can restore the fallen creation to new life and purpose.

Here's the logic of Scripture: The premise *only God can save* allows for no exceptions. So if it can be shown that the Father, the Son, and the Holy Spirit save, then all three will have to be recognized equally as God. Remember, the premise allows for no exceptions. If only God can save, and the Father saves by giving us all good things (James 1:17), then the Father is God. If only God can save, and Jesus the Son of God saves by defeating sin and death in his crucifixion and resurrection (2 Timothy 1:10), then Jesus is God. If only God can save and the Holy Spirit saves by giving us new life (John 6:63) and raising us from the dead (Romans 8:11), then the Spirit is God. If salvation comes from Father, Son, and Holy Spirit, then Father, Son, and Holy Spirit are equally God. It's that simple.

All of this means that the doctrine of God as a trinity is secure. The doctrine of the Trinity is not only shown in isolated verses of the New Testament; the *entire teaching* of Scripture about salvation demands it. Even if someone were to try to cast doubt on those isolated verses that support the deity of Jesus or the deity of the Holy Spirit, the overall logic of scriptural truth would still uphold the reality of God as a trinity (and ultimately show that the verses in question really do support the deity of the Son and the Spirit). I will show in the chapters that follow that the reality of the Trinity permeates all the pages of Scripture. Even the most imaginative heretic cannot remove it without ripping out every page of the Bible.

The insight that God is Father, Son, and Holy Spirit fundamentally informs the life of the church as well. In all of our songs, prayers, testimonies, and sermons, we express in one way or another the conviction that we receive all things from the hand of our heavenly Father through the one and only Son and in the power of the Holy Spirit. In the other direction, we receive all things within the life of the Holy Spirit, from Jesus, as granted ultimately by the heavenly Father. The Bible and the church encourage us to think of God the Savior as a trinity of persons: Father, Son, and Spirit. These three are the means by which God reaches us and we reach back. The path to the reality of God as trinity is well marked and clear once we know how to read the biblical map.

The problem is that the entire discussion that has occurred about the Trinity in the history of theology has made the map difficult to read. Theology has historically moved away from the events of the story of Jesus (and our experience of Christ) and increasingly in the direction of the more abstract issues of God's inner life (God's life apart from us or apart from history). A trend began in the Middle Ages to discuss the Trinity mainly within the more abstract issues of God's inner life. Theologians engaged in lengthy discussions about how to distinguish between the one nature and the three persons within the inner life of God. In the eleventh century, the church faced a centuries-long and growing tension over the issue of whether the Holy Spirit proceeds eternally (without beginning) from the Father alone, which the Eastern churches favored, or from the Father "and the Son" (*filioque* in Latin), which the Western churches connected to Rome preferred. The doctrine of the Trinity that was meant to help the believer make sense of the biblical story as well as the experience of salvation became instead mainly an intellectual puzzle in an effort to figure out the complexities of God's inner life.

Issues concerning God's inner life had their importance but not in isolation from the concrete story of Jesus featured in the Bible and experienced in the church. The concept of the Trinity was never meant to become merely an intellectual puzzle removed from the concrete issues of life. Theologians continued discussing the Trinity in separation from such concrete matters, leading the famous liberal theologian of the early nineteenth century Friederich Schleiermacher to decide that if the doctrine of the Trinity were to disappear from Christian doctrine, nothing would change in the slightest.

The great twentieth-century Swiss theologian Karl Barth sought to reverse this trend by showing that the doctrine of the Trinity is basic to our experience of the living Word of God in the proclamation of the church. Barth saw that the hearing of the Word of God through the preaching of the Scriptures in the church assumes that God is a divine trinity: the Father reveals the living Word (who is Christ) through "revealedness" or the power of revelation in us (which is the Holy Spirit). Since that time, theologians have elaborated on the doctrine of the Trinity even further, noting that God is a circle of love who saves us by taking us into a living communion of persons. By the Spirit we are taken into communion with Christ, and through Christ, with his heavenly Father.

Unfortunately, many people today still feel that the path to the doctrine of the Trinity in Scripture is unclear and unimportant, and they are far closer to Schleiermacher's views than to Barth's. The reality of the Trinity is rarely preached in the churches, and when it is, a common response is either a yawn or even a critical rejection. I have even heard people say that the topic should be ignored, since it is difficult to understand and leads to doctrinal debates and division. Meanwhile, God's identity as Father, Son, and Holy Spirit, which is so important to understanding the richness of Christian life and mission, remains neglected.

Think for a moment: Isn't it important to know that salvation occurs as the heavenly Father gives us the Spirit of the one and only Son, accepting us fully as part of the divine circle of love? Doesn't this view of salvation in the context of the Trinity sound richer than the mere focus traditionally placed on salvation as forgiveness or relief of guilt? Doesn't the notion of God as a trinity enrich our understanding of salvation and of the Christian life?

Such an understanding of God is sorely needed today. The twentieth century has come and gone, leaving us a legacy of unprecedented advances in science and technology. These advances have given us many wonderful possibilities for enhancing life. They have also given us scarred memories of massive destruction of human and nonhuman life, as well as the prospect of much more severe destruction. Many in this contemporary context have found it increasingly difficult to embrace the older idea of God as a distant ego who reigns from the heavens, imposing decisions unilaterally on the cosmos. Many have found the vision of God as a trinity of persons who form a circle of love a liberating idea in this new context. God is not a solitary ego removed from this world and reigning from on high, but is rather a circle of love, a communion of persons who have opened their shared life to a suffering world through the cross, the resurrection, and the bestowal of the Spirit. God still reigns on high but not in a way untouched by our shame and sorrow, not in a way removed from the core of life from which all things live and are renewed.

Interestingly, most Christians experience Father, Son, and Holy Spirit as the God who gives new life, without considering what this means. Who are these three players in the drama of salvation depicted in the Bible and how do they relate to each other towards the fulfillment of this drama? Let's turn again to the basic experience that all Christians share together of the Father, the Son, and the Holy Spirit, of all three as vital to salvation and, therefore, of all three as God.

We come to know the heavenly Father as the ultimate source of every good thing (James 1:17). We know Jesus, the Son, as the one who conquered sin and death on the cross and rose again to offer us a share in his new life (2 Timothy 1:10). We know the Holy Spirit as the power of new life that raised Jesus from the dead and that indwells us and brings us to the ultimate victory of life promised in the gospel (Romans 8:11). Again, if we experience the Father, the Son, and the Holy Spirit as essential to salvation, and if only God can save, the inescapable conclusion is that the Father, the Son, and the Spirit are all essentially divine, a trinity of persons that make up the one God.

My conviction is that the triune God is in fact the inescapable conclusion of the biblical premise that *only God can save*. We can then move from there to show how the notion of God as triune greatly enhances our understanding of the Christian life. I will illustrate further this necessity of logic with reference to a train ride that my wife, Verena, and I took once to what was then West Berlin.

West Berlin–Bound

It seems that our step-by-step journey guided by biblical truth concerning God's identity is not an uncertain or confusing path but rather a necessary and clear one, once its basic premise that *only God can save* is grasped. I am reminded here of a trip that my wife and I took to West Berlin during the mid-1980s while I was a doctoral student at a prominent Swiss university. The remainder of our trip was easy once we found our way by train to the East German border. Since the bulk of our trip took us through East Germany, the train to West Berlin did not allow for any detours or stops. Our train roared through station after station in East Germany without making a single stop. No one was able to exit the train or to choose another direction. In fact, these stations had East German guards walking along their platforms with weapons ready to be aimed at any unwanted intruders. Once we entered East Germany from our last station in West Germany, there was no exit until we reached our destination in West Berlin, which stood at that time like a little island in the middle of East Germany.

My point is that the step-by-step guide implied in Scripture to God's identity as a trinity of persons is a lot like the train ride that I just described. Metaphorically speaking, once we get on board at the basic premise that only God can save, we roar through the "stations" that indicate the deity of the Father, the Son, and then the Holy Spirit without being able to stop, get off, or take another direction. We are brought inescapably to the end station marked "the Trinity," and there is simply no other possible destination.

The overarching goal of this book is to take you as the reader through a detailed knowledge of the inescapable, step-by-step journey from the basic premise of Scripture (that only God can save) through to the conclusion of the journey (that God is eternally a loving and redemptive communion of Father, Son, and Holy Spirit). I have given readers a bird's-eye view of the map to our destination at the Trinitarian identity of God. In the pages that follow, I want to elaborate on the precise stations of the journey for the reader. There is a lot of Scripture to look at before I can convincingly make my case. I also realize that there are still many questions that can be asked about God's identity as a trinity and many conclusions to draw from this triune identity. I will attempt to deal with the major questions and conclusions towards the end of our study.

But before embarking at that important station from which our journey begins to discovering God's triune identity, I want to talk about the legitimacy of the Bible as the proper map. Most readers of this book may be convinced that the Bible is the only sure map to God's identity. But some may not be so sure. So before we discuss the points on the map, I want to establish the fact that the Bible is the only sure guide. This issue is important to discuss, since the force of logic throughout our discussion will only make sense once it is realized that we are following assumptions of *Scripture*. If left solely to the dictates of human religious imagination, there is no limit to the possibilities for determining God's identity. But once we bind our possibilities to the premises of Scripture, the logic of our journey emerges as set along a clear and necessary path. By the end of the book, the reader may indeed have to face the question of whether or not the scriptural path should be obeyed. So it is helpful to make the case right from the start as to why it is meaningful to decide in favor of obedience to the truth of Scripture.

Study Questions:

1. Looking carefully at Exodus 3:14 and 6:2–8, what does it mean to say that God is the "I AM WHO I AM"? Include in your answer the future orientation of this name.

2. Summarize how every event in the story of Jesus names God as Father, Son, and Holy Spirit.

3. How is God one and how is God three? Give scriptural proof for God's oneness and God's threeness.

4. What can be said to those who feel that the doctrine of the Trinity should be rejected because it is difficult to understand?

5. Explain the steps in logic that support the Trinity. Start with the basic premise and then explain why from there we must conclude that God is a trinity.

6. How has the history of the doctrine of the Trinity made the doctrine seem unnecessary?

7. What does the trip to West Berlin signify about the doctrine of the Trinity?

2
PREPARATIONS
Mapping the Trip

We cannot find the right destination without a good map. If we are taking a train, we also need an accurate train schedule. One mistake could cause us to take the wrong train and even to head in the wrong direction. The same is true analogously with finding our way to discovering who God is. There are an almost limitless number of maps available in the world for discovering God. Any number of religious sects and self-made prophets offer their own version of where to go and how to explore. It is the fundamental conviction of this book that the map of choice for journeying to God is the Bible. The entire logic following from the premise that only God can save proceeds along the lines of a reasoning that makes sense within the story of the Bible. Again and again we will note that the path taken must proceed in a certain direction because Scripture demands it.

Wouldn't it be great to possess a map that would take us to the identity, life, and actions of God? There is something inside all of us that yearns for this, for it would allow us to see beyond the veil of this world to the ultimate reality that explains the purpose of everything else. We yearn to know this ultimate mystery especially in times of crisis or great need. No matter what, there are always moments in which we are prone to think about it, even if we tend to suppress it by concentrating on the ordinariness of everyday life. Most of us just can't seem to avoid the desire to peer into this reality in order to see what, or rather *who*, it is. This desire is built into our spiritual DNA as the human race. It's the kind of question we were made to ask.

God: The Unavoidable Question

The God question (or question about God's existence and identity) is unavoidable. It grabs us when we least expect it, even after we have done everything we could to avoid it. The Psalmist wrote to God, "Where can I go from your Spirit?" (Psalm 139:7). This is a rhetorical question, the implied answer being "nowhere." God seems unavoidable. Even as we seek to flee, we run into God wherever we go. The Bible says this is because we draw our very breath from God (Acts 17:25) and "in him we live and move and have our being" (Acts 17:28). So how can we escape the reality of God if our own humanity depends on God's presence for its very vitality? The God question poses itself to us because without it we ourselves remain an unanswered question. When we ask the question concerning who we are, we need the God answer to answer it.

Sometimes the God question comes to us in a deeply moving way. I still recall stepping late one evening into my backyard as a teenager who was still striving to avoid making an adult commitment to God. I had done everything I could to run from God. The weather was mild with a cool breeze, typical of autumn evenings in the Midwest. The stars were unusually visible that night, providing me with a rare glimpse of the beauty of creation. Suddenly, a falling star caught my eye to my left. I stood fixated on the sky, captivated by the sight before me. I seem to have lost track of the time as I stared at the magnificent beauty before me. The question suddenly came to me: "Who is God?" I didn't wonder whether there was a God, but rather who this God *was*.

The existence of God has never been a source of anguish for me. God's existence has always been for me a given. I was never able to imagine my life or the vast cosmos without something grander to account for it. I have never been able to imagine life except as a gift granted by a higher source. Psalm 19:1–2 tells us that the universe declares its dependence on God as its source: "The heavens declare the glory of God; the skies proclaim the work of his hands. Day after day they pour forth speech; night after night they display knowledge." The Apostle Paul even goes so far as to say that God's awesome power and deity are "clearly seen" in nature so that people are forced to "suppress" this truth in order to deny it (Romans 1:18–20). Acts 17 implies that an intuition of God's existence is already built into our lives as mortal beings. This chapter notes that we were made to search for God even though the divine presence is not far from all of us. From God we draw our mortal breath and in God we live and move and have our being. How ironic that the God we implicitly yearn for and grope after is already so near to us as to provide us with our very breath and vitality. God is more vital to life than we could ever imagine.

As I stared into the sky that night, I wondered again, "Who is this God who lives beyond the stars? Who is this God embracing me and seeking to draw me in? Who is this God who is so vast and far but also so deep and near? This God must be the most fascinating personal being ever." Thinking back, I'm reminded of the fact that the God of Genesis 1 who created the universe by the spoken word seems transcendent and limitless in power. Yet this very same God can condescend to walk in a garden and to call out to Adam (Genesis 3:8–9). God is calling us, too. Will we answer? Our lives will remain an unanswered question until we do.

That evening I spent staring up at the sky played a role in my eventual commitment to Jesus Christ, which I made after an all-night conversation with my father. I was eighteen and fresh out of high school. I informed my father that I wanted to travel across America to find myself. That led to an all-night conversation, in which he read Scriptures to me about God's desire to draw me into the divine love and will for me. He told me stories of what God had done for our family over the years; some of them I had heard before, but they all spoke to me that night as though I was hearing them for the first time. I held out and would not make a commitment to Christ as the dawn broke. I returned exhausted to my room, and I recall vividly the impression that I had. I could not run from God any longer, for to do so would mean that I would run from something that was already a part of me, a valued and vital part of who I was and was meant to be. I recall praying to the effect that I could no longer run. I asked God to "take my life." Since that moment, one of my favorite hymns has been "Take My Life and Let It Be" (lyrics by Frances Havergal). It was sung at my wedding.

There are four different ways that we were created to inquire after God (or to implicitly ask the question about the reality of God). We have been made to ask the God question in four ways. First, we were made to reflect the divine *image*. Genesis 1:27 states that Adam and Eve were made "in the image of God." What this means precisely has been debated among theologians for centuries. The essential meaning is given to us in the very next verse (1:28), which notes that the first pair were created to partner together in order to procreate (fill the earth with their progeny) and to exercise wise and loving lordship (or stewardship) over the creation. Such tasks of proliferating life and managing it require loving and respectful partnerships as well as intelligence, creativity, and a hopeful vision for the future—all qualities that mimic those that belong to God as a loving communion of Father, Son, and Holy Spirit. Humanity has not continued to honor life or to care for the creation. We have created instead a "culture of death" and continue to both victimize and be victimized by it. But this is not why we were created. We were made to mimic God in proliferating and caring for life in a trustful relationship with God. We cannot understand the purpose for which we were made until we discover this.

Second, we were made to bear within us the Holy Spirit of God, to be God's unique dwelling place in creation. Genesis 2:7 says that God breathed the divine breath or Spirit into Adam and he became a living soul. The soul is not God's breath, but the soul came into being through God's breath or Spirit, and lives from the Spirit. Moreover, the Spirit is meant to dwell within to sanctify us by separating us from sin and consecrating us to God, empowering us to live for God. This Holy Spirit also gives us a share in God's immortality or life eternal (2 Corinthians 5:1–5). But the first human pair disobeyed God and resisted the Spirit's indwelling, becoming enslaved by sin and death. We still draw our breath and vitality from the Spirit (Acts 17:25–28), but the Spirit does not dwell within humanity to sanctify and consecrate within the bounds of saving grace. Humanity will not rediscover its meaning and purpose until it discovers God and receives the Spirit within once more. Until then, we implicitly yearn for God.

Third, we were made to be brothers and sisters of Jesus Christ, God's one and only Son. All things were made *by and for* Jesus (Colossians 1:16). Creation was made as God's household, God's dwelling place. God's one and only Son was meant to have preeminence within this household as its Redeemer and Lord (Colossians 1:15–18). But when he came into the world, the world did not recognize him. God's chosen people who had been prepared for centuries by God to be his welcoming committee did not recognize him (John 1:10–11). But he was still ordained of the Father to be "the firstborn among many" brothers and sisters (Romans 8:29), the firstborn from the dead, the first to be resurrected from mortality to immortality (Colossians 1:18).

Last, we were made to hear from God's inspired Word and obey it. This Word is first Jesus Christ (John 1:14) and it is also the sacred Scriptures, which are able to make us wise unto salvation through faith in Christ (2 Timothy 3:15–16). We drink from this Word like newborn babies drink milk from their mothers, because this Word is sustenance to our souls and necessary to our growth (1 Peter 2:2–3). God spoke all creation into existence by the divine Word (Genesis 1) and God's inspired Word will continue to be the means by which we find our way towards the future that God has for us. This Word is the eternal seed planted in us from which we are born anew as children of God (1 Peter 1:23). Faith is born from this Word and grows from it (Romans 10:17).

The God question is thus tied deeply to the existence of all of us, even those who may not usually be conscious of it. This question is indeed driven by more than idle curiosity. If everything came from God (James 1:17; Hebrews 11:3), then the meaning and final purpose of everything must be connected to God in some deep and intimate way. This is why the question never leaves us. Both God and we remain mysteries this side of eternity for both the novice and the mature in the faith. In a way, our search for God is also a search for ourselves, and suppressing the truth about God suppresses something vital about who we are. Exploring who God is uncovers something essential to my own background, heritage, and future hope. Like it or not, I and everyone else are inseparably connected to God, and to each other because of God. I simply cannot avoid asking the question of who this God is, and I deny something important about myself if

I fail to ask it. But how can I discover who God is and what God is most like? Where do I look?

God Is Self-Defining

Though we naturally yearn for God and have some general intuitions about God, we cannot from our own resources discover who God is exactly. The only place to look for such understanding, ultimately, is God. To use a human comparison, if someone wants to know who I am, the best thing to do is to come to *me,* or at least to learn about what I have said and done to introduce myself. The same is certainly true of God. So the first thing we must say is that God must be the decisive source of any answer concerning who God is. Another way of saying this is that God is *self-defining.* The right to be self-defining is essential to the dignity and freedom of all persons. I would never tolerate stepping into a community of people I've never met before only to have them tell me who I am based largely on their intuitions, expectations, and desires. No one would ever tolerate that, so why should we expect God to tolerate it?

Besides, do we really think that we have the capacity in our own abilities to reach God and to figure out God for ourselves? Such a presumption is outlawed by the Bible as the sin of the tower of Babel (Genesis 11). The narrative of the tower of Babel tells us that the original inhabitants of Babel attempted to build a tower to God in order to make a name for themselves (Genesis 11:4). God judged them by confusing their languages and dispersing them throughout the earth. This actually fulfilled the original mandate given to humanity to populate the earth (Genesis 1:28). Acts 17:26–27 informs us that God dispersed the peoples throughout the earth that they might take the *divinely-chosen* path, rather than their own self-centered one, to the divine mystery. We can't reach God; God must reach us. If we seek after and find God, it is only because God has found us and led us in the path of discovery.

Let's face it, humanity's intuition about God is not extensive and is subject to distortion. We have expectations about who God should be, based on social conditioning, rumor, misunderstood personal experiences, and personal idiosyncrasies, and then we've formulated a mental picture of God based on these. Consequently, some think God is a kill-joy who has figured out all of the ways in which we can have fun or pleasure and then outlawed them. Others think of God as an old man who is always serious and is angry most of the time. We torture ourselves with such thoughts. In the service of self-gratification, some might think of God as a cosmic Santa who gives us whatever we lay claim to. When God doesn't live up to our expectations, we are quick to place blame or express deep disappointment. Unconditional obedience to God's lordship is replaced in this case by self-preoccupation. Self-made ideas about God are distortions because they arise from our own imaginations. They crowd out more than reveal God. They don't allow God to be self-revealing.

God is infinitely greater than anything we could possibly imagine. God says in Isaiah 40:25, "To whom will you compare me? Or who is my equal?" God is utterly unique and not to be compared to our self-made idols. As sinful beings, we have the deplorable tendency to make idols and to call them "God." We are all the more dependent on God's power of self-disclosure because we are finite and fallen, unable to discern spiritual matters in our own power (1 Corinthians 2:14). Although we do have some intuitions about God implied by nature, there is plenty of room for us to distort these, and we do so to some extent all of the time.

This is why God condemns idolatry, or the making of images fashioned after our own fetishes and designed to bring God into our grasp on our own (self-serving) terms (Exodus 20:4–5). The mystery of God and of God's free self-disclosure must be respected. This respect implies that we will accept God's revelation and obey it, even if it shatters long-cherished expectations. As Paul wrote, "Oh, the depth of the riches of the wisdom and knowledge of God! How unsearchable his judgments, and his paths beyond tracing out! 'Who has known the mind of the Lord? Or who has been his counselor?' 'Who has ever given to God, that God should repay him?' For from him and through him and to him are all things. To him be the glory forever! Amen" (Romans 11:33–36).

Notice the above phrase "from him and through him and to him are all things." This phrase is implicitly Trinitarian. Read it again like this: "From him (God the Father) and through him (Jesus Christ and the Holy Spirit) and to him (back to the Father via the Holy Spirit and Christ) are all things." Yes, all things come from the heavenly Father through Christ our mediator and in the presence of the Holy Spirit, and all things proceed from the Holy Spirit and through Christ back to God the Father. Notice also that the triune God is not bound to human expectations. Our text above says, "Who has ever given to God that God should repay him?" This God is free and sovereign, unreachable by human power and uncontrolled by human schemes.

This principle of divine freedom and mystery is found in the Bible from the beginning. As I noted in my last chapter, God informed Moses in Exodus 3 of the divine plan to deliver the Israelites from Egyptian bondage. Then Moses asked for God's name. With this question, Moses asked for more than a formal introduction, since names in the ancient world revealed something vital about a person's character, commitments, or plans. God's answer is telling. God said to Moses, "I AM WHO I AM" (Exodus 3:14). Scholars of this text often point out that a possible translation might also be "I will be what I will be." On the one hand, this statement implies that God is *self-revealing*. God will be to Israel what God will be (or God will be revealed in accordance with what God wishes to reveal and has promised in freedom to reveal). The Israelites will need to wait to see what will be revealed concerning who God is. On the other hand, God is faithful to be what God has determined to be, what God has promised to be. Exodus 6 grants us specific promises of how God will be revealed as Lord in the exodus event. That "God is what God has determined to be" or that "God will be to Israel what God will be" are both implied by "I am who I am."

This principle of God's right to be self-revealing extends throughout time and is not confined to the deliverance of Israel from bondage in Egypt. It includes not just the exodus of Israel from bondage but also the words of the prophets and especially the crucifixion and resurrection of Jesus Christ for our salvation. The key event in God's self-disclosure is the resurrection of Jesus, because there God reveals that he is Lord of salvation, the only Savior. God defeats sin, death, and the powers of darkness to reign supreme over all. This God is Lord of life whose breath creates and renews life, even glorifies it beyond the bounds of mortal existence.

This God is thus the only one who conquers sin and death and offers hope in the darkest hour. God said in Ezekiel 37:13, "Then you, my people, will know that I am the LORD, when I open your graves and bring you up from them." This was the faith of Abraham long ago, for even he believed "the God who gives life to the dead and calls things that are not as though they were" (Romans 4:17). Such was fulfilled in the resurrection of Christ, which stands as the ultimate revelation of God as Lord of salvation.

Indeed, Christ is the "full[ness] of grace and truth" (John 1:14), the radiance of God's glory and the exact representation of God's being (Hebrews 1:3). Indeed, the resurrection of Jesus is that place where God's deity and blazing glory are revealed. Of course, God's deity and glory are also shown in the crucifixion, where God humbled

himself to be bruised and crushed on our behalf through the crucified body of Jesus. But without the resurrection, we would not have
known for sure that it was God the Lord of salvation there. It is in the
resurrection that the revelation of God in Christ reaches its decisive
point of fulfillment.

From the lens of the risen Christ, we can see how God's self-
disclosure also includes the outpouring of the Holy Spirit at Pentecost
(where the power of the risen life enters us), the witness of Scripture
(which points to the risen Christ and is validated by him), and the
perfection of the Spirit's work throughout creation in witness to Christ
when the dead are raised and the old creation is made new (which is
where the resurrection of Christ has its full effect in creation). God
will be fully disclosed in ultimate glory when he makes everything
new (Revelation 21:5). In the meantime, the question of who God
is remains a vital one and the standard of discernment is the Bible,
because the Bible bears witness to all that God has done to be introduced to humanity, especially in the context of the risen Christ.

Reading the Right Map

We may not have anything available exactly like a road map to
God, but we do have a sacred text called the Bible. The Bible is called
a *canon* (which means "standard"), because it serves to test and to
guide our speech about God and our acts of obedience. Paul said it
best when writing to Timothy that "all Scripture is God-breathed and
is useful for teaching, rebuking, correcting and training in righteousness" (2 Timothy 3:16). Notice this reference to the Scriptures as
"God-breathed." Just as human words require breath to be spoken, so
too did Scripture come to us on the winds of God's breath and is still
spoken to our hearts by this same breath, a figurative depiction of the

Holy Spirit. Let those who have an ear hear what the Spirit is saying to the churches (Revelation 2:29).

What is implied by the verse in 2 Timothy is that the Bible is the primary or privileged voice that speaks on behalf of the Holy Spirit in the churches. I don't mean to say that the Spirit dictated to the biblical authors what they should write. The very different writing styles and theological accents of the various biblical books and passages have caused dictation theories to lose their force as viable explanations of the role of the Spirit in inspiring Scripture. It seems clear that the human authors contributed to their writings from various influences arising from their cultures and personalities. But the general guidance of the Spirit on the writing of Scripture does mean that the Spirit guided what was written and then stood behind it, giving it the divine stamp of approval. So if we want to know what the Spirit wants to say to the churches or beyond, we must look first to the Scriptures. True, the Spirit can speak to our hearts and through many different forms of human communication. But all forms of human witness that claim to speak on behalf of God must speak in harmony with this inspired biblical text, for this text is "God-breathed" as the privileged voice of the Spirit in the churches.

Again, make no mistake about it, the Bible was written by ancient human authors who wrote from within struggles and issues facing their lives and believing communities. Their writings are embedded in the authors' ancient cultures and their witness to God reflects those realities. Yet their witness is not the mere product of ancient human efforts to understand God. In fact, their major theme is not various human efforts to understand God but rather God's message to humanity. The main burden of their writings was to bear witness to miraculous events and inspired communications from God that tell us what God has done for us and wishes to say to us.

Even very human prayers to God in the Psalms that reveal human weakness are transformed into God's Word to us as they are read in the churches and properly interpreted in a way that is faithful to Christ, for the biblical writers themselves in bearing witness "spoke from God as they were carried along by the Holy Spirit" (2 Peter 1:21). The skilled interpreter will seek to discern God's liberating message for us today from the Bible's ancient human witness. The fact that the Bible was inspired of God when it was written means that God guided the authors of Scripture so that the divine message would be faithfully presented. That the Bible is still inspired by the same Spirit means that this message is applicable and life-transforming among us as well.

The question that I commonly get from students has to do with how I know that the Bible is the inspired Word of God. Can I say something more than that the Holy Spirit uses it to witness to Christ and to transform lives today? Well, this *is* a good place to start. The Bible proves itself to be God's Word by leading us to the risen Christ who is able to save. Before telling Timothy that all Scripture is God-breathed, Paul reminded him of how "you have known the holy Scriptures, which are able to make you wise for salvation through faith in Christ Jesus" (2 Timothy 3:15). Timothy was in deep fear and self-doubt about his ability to fulfill his calling as a minister (2 Timothy 1:3–7), so Paul reminded Timothy of the power of the Scriptures through the work of the Spirit to give him all that he needed to bring people to Christ (3:15–17). Paul noted that the Scriptures fulfill this role because they are inspired (literally, "God-breathed") by the Holy Spirit (3:16).

Think of the matter in this way: If someone were to ask, "How do you know that a treasure map is authentic?" a satisfactory answer would certainly be, "It has led me to the treasure." In a sense, we say the same thing to those who wonder how we as Christians know that the Bible is God's Word. It has led us to the treasure of salvation that is hidden in the risen Christ.

To people who have not yet found Christ in the pages of Scripture, we would ask them to come to this text in order to "taste and see that the LORD is good" (Psalm 34:8). Paul wrote to the Corinthians that a veil covers the hearts of those who read the Old Testament (old covenant) Scriptures, and added concerning this veil that "it has not been removed, because only in Christ is it taken away" (2 Corinthians 3:14). Through the agency of the Holy Spirit, the risen Christ authenticates Scripture as God's Word by removing the veil of misunderstanding and saving those who turn to him in faith when reading the message of the Bible.

Someone might object at this point that we are authenticating Scripture as the Word of God too much through experience. Can human testimonies of religious experience be trusted? Couldn't the same be said of a sacred text belonging to any religion? Don't devotees of all religions claim to have had life-changing experiences from their sacred texts? What makes the Bible any different?

Here is where it is important to add three points. First, the argument from experience is not to be underestimated. People nowadays want to know that the chosen path to discovering God is real in the concrete sense that it will make a tangible difference in life. Academic arguments alone will not convince. Moreover, I don't deny that other texts besides the Bible have some truth in them and can be used of the Spirit to create a thirst for God and (implicitly) for Christ. That some valid experience of God is possible outside of the Bible cannot be denied, even if it is not entirely accurately explained by those who have had it. My point is not that the Bible is the *only* avenue of the Spirit's voice; I mean that, validated by the risen Christ, the Bible is the *privileged* voice of the Spirit that functions as the standard for judging all other experiences.

Second, we are not just talking about experience in and of itself but rather about the living Christ who encounters us in the pages of this text. It is not just the aesthetic or emotional appeal of the biblical story nor is it the influence of my religious community that is making this text come alive in my mind and heart. It is rather the living Christ himself through the power of the Spirit that proves this text to be the authentic path to God. Though Christ is *experienced* in Scripture, Christ is more than an experience. Christ is the living Lord who, as God, conquered sin and death for us.

Third, Christ's authentication of the Scriptures does not only take place within the experience of the individual believer or the believing community. It also occurred objectively and historically with dramatic implications. The Jewish Scriptures (our Old Testament) pointed to Christ through a rich array of types and prophetic messages about the coming Messiah. Some of these are detailed, such as naming the actual place where the Messiah would be born, namely Bethlehem (Micah 5:2).

Some of these prophetic passages seem on the surface to contradict one another until they are viewed in the light of Christ. Daniel 7:13–14 implies that the coming Messiah (called a "son of man") will receive from God full divine authority to reign forever over God's *eternal* kingdom and that this Messiah will himself be *worshiped* as divine. Yet Isaiah 53 states that the coming Messiah will be *despised*, considered smitten of God, led as a lamb to the slaughter, and will appear to have no majesty or glory. In fact, he will be *cut off* and his lineage will be nonexistent. These two passages seem to contradict each other until viewed in the light of Christ's crucifixion and resurrection. In his life and death, Christ is the suffering servant despised and cut off, considered smitten of God for our salvation (Isaiah 53; see Mark 10:45). But in his resurrection, ascension, and coming reign, he is also the glorious Son of Man, worshiped as divine and given the charge to reign over God's eternal kingdom (Daniel 7:13–14; see Matthew 28:18; Acts 1:9, 2:33). Who else in history so wonderfully harmonized through fulfillment these two seemingly inconsistent prophecies?

The Old Testament Scripture is like a puzzle with the center pieces missing. No other figure in history fits these missing slots except Christ. Placing him there, we are moved by how well he fits. Moreover, when Christ was raised from the dead, there remained no doubt that he was the one foretold as the coming Savior in the Old Testament. After all, as we noted above, God predicted that he would be revealed one day as the Lord of salvation by raising the dead (Ezekiel 37:13).

Moreover, Christ himself noted that he was the one who would fulfill the Old Testament, every aspect of it from the law to the prophets (Matthew 5:17–18). After his resurrection, it became clear to Jesus' disciples that he had in fact fulfilled the Old Testament. Christ then appointed these disciples as apostles to govern his church, promising that the Holy Spirit whom he would give to them would lead them into all truth concerning what Christ taught and did (John 16:13). The preaching and witness of the apostles then shaped the writings of the New Testament.

The risen Christ stands historically at the center of the Bible as its chief point of validation as God's Word. In his resurrection he fulfilled and validated the Old Testament as God's Word and, by giving such illumination by the Spirit to his apostles, he indirectly validated what went into the New Testament. The Bible points to Christ and Christ validates the Bible both objectively in history and subjectively (and intersubjectively) in the life experience of communities of faith everywhere and throughout time.

All of this makes the Scriptures the authentic map for discovering who God is. How do we know that the Scriptures are God's Word? They lead to Christ and Christ points to them as the faithful guide.

How do we know that a treasure map is authentic? It points the way to the treasure and the treasure, once found, validates the map as authentic.

All of this is not to say that the Bible is a set of maps written by the finger of God, but I would maintain that the Bible does give us genuine insight into the identity and works of God. It is as close as we can get to reading God's maps this side of eternity. Through the work of the Holy Spirit, the risen Christ can be embraced in the pages of this text and, through him, the redemptive will of the heavenly Father. This is the text that shows us where and how God has been introduced and identified. In God's self-identification in the Scriptures, we can best see who God is and what this God is like. This canon is the place where we go again and again to listen and to obey, to test our experiences, prophetic utterances, and acts of obedience and to discover the meaning of the gospel for our time and place. Those among us with the ministry of oversight (such as pastors) will seek to bring us all again and again to the voices of this text with the goal of hearing the mind of God and discovering ever more deeply who God is.

Sound Doctrine: The Steps of Biblical Reasoning

The Bible is different from a set of maps in another way—it is more complex. Though its basic message has a delightful simplicity to it, the medium of this message (the biblical text itself) requires careful interpretation. A difficulty that we face in elevating the biblical text as a source of guidance is in the fact that the biblical message is diversely expressed and scattered throughout the biblical canon. In places it is implied within texts that require careful interpretation to unearth it. The Bible spans many pages as well as many cultures and eras of time. It involves narrative, poetry, prophecy, and epistles. It involves a diversity of voices and lines of argument, some of which exist in creative tension with one another. I do not deny the wonderful harmony and unity of this book, but many things are clear only through careful study.

Fortunately, the church has not been without guidance in its discernment of the biblical message concerning God and what God has done for us. The Holy Spirit has helped the church at key points in its history, especially in the early centuries of the church's history, to arrive at doctrinal formulations that capture the essence of what the Bible teaches on vital areas of concern. Doctrine is not the only means by which the Spirit has helped the church be faithful to the biblical message, but it has become the most authoritative in the life of the church. Doctrines carefully crafted from Scripture have helped us historically by offering us summary statements of truth that clarify the essential message of the Bible and that speak to new challenges facing the church. Doctrines like salvation by grace, the deity of Christ, and the reality of the Trinity have helped to summarize for the church essential biblical truths. All major branches of the Christian church stand behind these truths. One of the purposes of this book will be to explore how the Bible makes these truths a necessary part of the church's understanding of truth.

Doctrine is in fact as old as the Bible itself. Titus 1:9 speaks of a Christian leader as someone who must "hold firmly to the trustworthy message as it has been taught, so that he can encourage others by sound doctrine and refute those who oppose it." Doctrine has always played an important role in the life of the church in keeping followers of Christ faithful to the biblical message. Doctrine can be said to aid the Scriptures in regulating the church's speech to and about God, like grammar regulates our use of a language. Some, therefore, refer to doctrine as the "grammar of faith."

Of course, doctrines arrived at in the history of the church are not inspired like the Bible is, which is why they must constantly be tested by the voices of Scripture and restated in each new context and time period in ways that are relevant to fresh questions. And not all doctrines carry the same weight. Those that are expressed in the foundational creeds of the church (like the Apostles' Creed or Nicene Creed—crafted in the early centuries of the church before the church was divided) deal with such vital issues as salvation by grace and Christ's deity, and have been held as most important. These doctrines are called *dogma*, because they are considered most essential to the church's faithfulness to the biblical message. But not all doctrines are as vital to the church's witness. For example, the doctrine of footwashing as an ordinance is cherished in some churches but not in most. Even if we regard this doctrine as valid, we have to admit that it is not as vital to the church as the deity of Christ.

Sound doctrine guides us in our process of discerning who God is and what God has done for us. It helps to guide how we worship and speak about God, helping to keep our speech faithful to the canon of Scripture. Though doctrine is also sensitive to worship and the cultural realities and challenges that the church faces in the world, doctrine has its base in the witness of Scripture.

This issue of base reminds me of the base leg of a statue. Archeologists tell us that ancient statues typically had a base leg and a bent or free leg. The base leg typically provided the statue with its strength and foundation. I like to think that sound doctrine has its base leg in Scripture and its free leg in its cultural context in the world as well as the church's missionary life. In its role in regulating the church's speech to and about God, doctrine is primarily based in Scripture. Since doctrines are not perfect, they must continuously be tested by their foundation in Scripture and explained in ways that are relevant to each new generation and for different cultural contexts. The challenge is in keeping the faithful witness of doctrine essentially unaltered even as it finds fresh forms of expression.

There have historically been five major doctrines considered to be most essential to the Christian faith. These are the doctrines that speak the most clearly to us concerning who God is and what God has done for us. As noted in our last chapter, these doctrines are based on a simple premise that is widely accepted among God's people as foundational to the biblical message—namely, that only God can save.

1. Only the one God who created all things can save.
2. The heavenly Father is divine since the Father is the source of all life and saves through the Son and the Holy Spirit.
3. Jesus Christ as the one and only Son of the Father is divine because he saves by conquering death and granting new life through the agency of the Holy Spirit.
4. The Holy Spirit is divine because the Spirit perfects salvation by making all things new, in the Son and to the glory of the Father.
5. God is the Trinity, an interactive communion of love consisting of Father, Son, and Holy Spirit.

The point that I wish to stress throughout this book is that each of the five steps involved in this doctrinal heritage are interconnected and essential to all of the rest. Once we acknowledge the first point (that only God can save), the deity of the Father, Son, and Holy Spirit fall naturally into place beneath as necessary and logical outcomes. This is because all three save in interaction with each other. If only God can save, and these three save in interaction with each other, then these three are divine: the one God is an interactive communion of three persons. It's the role of doctrine to clarify this biblical reasoning, the reasoning of faith and worship. Sound doctrine allows the church to reason step by step through to the larger picture of who God is. Christians who find doctrines like salvation, the deity of Christ, and the Trinity puzzling need to understand more about the scriptural logic that has led the church from one of these points to the others.

The result of treading this path of biblical reasoning can be surprising and deeply rewarding. Many of my students rejoice at the idea that God is not a solitary ego ruling the universe from a far-away throne but is rather a rich communion of love among persons. Many are also enlightened by the idea that salvation is not just forgiveness or the relief of guilt but is also an entry into a loving communion between the heavenly Father and the Son that was sent to redeem us, enjoyed by the Holy Spirit. What we are speaking of here is not just an exercise in logic for the sake of intellectual clarity (as important as this is) but also a life-transforming discovery through scriptural doctrine of who God is. Let's continue, for we have only scratched the surface. There is much more to discuss about how the Bible leads us step by step to the reality of God as the Trinity.

Study Questions:

1. Why is the God question unavoidable? Include the ways in which we have been made for God.

2. Why is it important to allow God to be self-defining?

3. Explain the phrase "from him and through him and to him are all things" taken from Romans 11:33–36.

4. According to 2 Timothy 3:15–16, how do we know that the Bible is the Word of God?

5. What does it mean to say that Christ and the Scriptures are mutually authenticating?

6. How did I respond to those who may say that my discussion makes the authority of the Bible too dependent on experience?

7. What is the role of sound doctrine in relation to Scripture?

3
STATION ONE
Only God Can Save

We've just arrived at the first station of our journey. It has a sign that reads "Only God Can Save!" After having prepared for our journey by establishing that the Bible is our guide to God's identity, we should look carefully at what it teaches or, in our train metaphor, to the stations to which it points for the journey. As I mentioned before, there is a basic premise to Scripture—namely, that only God the Creator can save the creation; only the one who created life can breathe new life into it to save and renew it. To put it more concisely, *only God can save*. This simple statement seems so obvious that it hardly needs to be said. Yet there are numerous reasons why this must be said and confirmed by the voices of Scripture. For one thing, this brief statement has been the chief guiding principle in the steps that the church has taken historically in arriving at its key doctrinal statements about God. With every step of doctrine concerning God, the church has seemed to be saying, "If only God can save, then . . ." For example, "If only God can save, then we cannot save ourselves by our own works." And, "If only God can save, then Christ must be divine in order to be recognized as our Savior," and so on.

Before we get on board at this station, we should understand it better. Let's linger here for a moment. Before we proceed any further, we need to explain what we mean by salvation. I also think we need to establish more fully the fact that the Scriptures do support the notion that only God can save.

Salvation? From What?

I'll never forget an experience that I had as a college student leading an evangelism team for an evening of what we used to call "street evangelism"—that is, going out on a Friday or Saturday evening to the downtown area of our town to talk to folks (mostly young people hanging out) about Jesus Christ. I vividly recall sharing my personal testimony about Jesus Christ with someone. He was a young college student like me except he seemed angry at the world, especially the church. As soon as I used the word *saved* (that Christ saved me from my sins), he scoffed at the word. "Salvation!" he yelled. "What is that?!"

Before I had the chance to answer, he continued as though giving me instruction. "First, the church convinces you that you're lower than dirt. Then," he continued, "they set you up to do whatever they want you to do, because they exalt themselves as your only hope, a salvation machine! They have you just where they want you!" His arms were spread wide and he was leaning towards me with a scowl on his face for emphasis.

I tried to explain to him that churches may at times try to function this way, but that is no proof that the need for salvation doesn't still exist. I tried to share with him how lost and purposeless I was without

Christ in the world, but he remained unconvinced. He then told me a story of how he attended church once with his uncle, only to hear more about money and membership responsibilities than anything else. "They only want your cash and for that they give you a crutch to lean on—that is, if you're weak minded." I still recall his stressing how Christianity was for the "weak minded."

Again, I tried to show him that although churches can sometimes function in negative ways to offer unnecessary "crutches," what I was talking about was something deeper. I was referring to the need for God that is deep at the core of our lives as fallen beings in need of freedom and purpose. He just kept shaking his head, as if saying to me, "I'm not ready to hear you." I left feeling frustrated and exhausted. My only comfort was the fact that I had faithfully planted a seed. The rest was to be God's work. I would like to think that what I said eventually made a difference to him. I believe that God was not finished with that young man and may have broken through to him at some future point in his life. I hope so.

My story illustrates that there are a lot of folks who may or may not believe in the existence of God and who find talk about the need for salvation to be annoying and utter nonsense. They are convinced that they are doing quite well on their own and that life is not really so bad after all. Life will naturally have its ups and downs. It will have its beauty and its ugliness, its joy and its sorrow. Why introduce a notion of salvation into the meaning of life? Why does anyone need to be saved anyway? Isn't this alleged need for salvation fabricated by organized religion in its attempt to gain power and influence over people's lives? Isn't it just another way of inducing fear and forcing obedience among people so that they'll give money to organized religion and do what the leaders of religious sects tell them to do?

Well, there is no doubt that organized religion can be known to use fear and intimidation to manipulate people in certain cases. But this has nothing directly to do with whether or not salvation is really needed. Nevertheless, salvation continues to be ridiculed in the media, from movies to late-night comedians. The image of the preacher calling down hellfire and brimstone in front of naïve audiences who respond by calling out to be saved is still used to mock all legitimate appeals to the need for salvation. But is the need for salvation really so funny?

Interestingly, many in our society who might scoff at the idea of salvation will spend enormous amounts of money and time seeking their own version of it. We build huge armies and defense systems to protect ourselves from death at the hands of foreign enemies, not to mention billions of dollars on crime prevention and homeland security to protect ourselves from local threats. We spend billions on scientific (and pseudo-scientific) efforts to prolong life and to reverse the effects of aging. We spend billions on space exploration fueled in part by the idea that other planets might one day provide a refuge if our planet becomes for some reason uninhabitable. We spend billions on various forms of therapy in hopes that we can bring peace to our troubled souls or to mend broken and graceless relationships. Self-help books are national bestsellers. The human quest for personal welfare and even immortality is as old as the human race. At least some of these efforts are necessary and noble. But what astounds me is the vigor and passion that is expended towards some form of deliverance from death, guilt, gracelessness, or meaninglessness. It seems that the quest for some sort of salvation is not so nonsensical or funny after all. Could it be that there is really something inside of us that yearns for what Christ has to offer?

It is in the context of this discussion that we can talk about the need for salvation, except we refer here to a salvation that only God can offer and that really and truly lasts. The human quest for welfare, peace, and even immortality reflects something profound that humans seem to intuit. Human beings feel the weight of sin and death and intuitively try to shed it like an old coat. The problem is that we cannot get rid of these things. They hold us captive because they permeate creation. We delude ourselves if we think that we can shed them by our own power. The desire to shed them, however, is in some sense noble, since it shows that we were not made for these things and we resist allowing them to ultimately define us.

We were made for life and peace, as well as for justice, love, and hope. Paul wrote that we are made for immortality and life as God grants them through the Holy Spirit. We implicitly groan and strive within for this new "tent," or set of clothes: "For while we are in this tent, we groan and are burdened, because we do not wish to be unclothed but to be clothed with our heavenly dwelling, so that what is mortal may be swallowed up by life. Now it is God who has made us for this very purpose and has given us the Spirit as a deposit, guaranteeing what is to come" (2 Corinthians 5:4–5).

This text tells us that we are made for the immortal life that comes from the everlasting God. It implies that sin and death were not part of God's intention for us and that these conditions of human existence came into being as a result of our failure to trust in God and our desire to pave our own path apart from him. We fell into gracelessness and sin; we were overtaken by death and forces of darkness. Yet we remain in the very image and likeness of God (Genesis 1:27; 5:1). There is something in us that still yearns for freedom from sin and its effects in life. There is something still in us that yearns for life, and not just biological or material life, for humanity was not made to "live on bread alone" (Matthew 4:4). We yearn for spiritual and eternal life in communion with God. It is the divine breath that sparked the birth of humans as living souls (Genesis 2:7), and it is through a return to the divine Spirit that we are fulfilled once more.

Salvation is not such a strange concept once we notice how deeply we implicitly yearn for it. Here's the rub, however: it cannot be had by the human race through mere human effort and accomplishment. Salvation is through the restoration of a lost relationship with God as Creator and Lord. New life and immortality come only as a gift from God the Creator. It is simply not something we can do for ourselves. We did not create ourselves; neither can we save ourselves or raise ourselves from the dead. Only the Creator who made us can forgive us, restore us, and raise us from the death that holds us captive. The Bible is the story of how God did this through Christ and the sending of the Holy Spirit. Though we must use the grace that God gives us to receive this salvation, salvation comes from God alone.

Only God Can Save: A Biblical Premise

The Old Testament Scriptures reveal that the Israelites were reminded on more than one occasion that they should acknowledge no God but the Creator and Redeemer who rescued them from bondage in Egypt and formed a covenant with them by grace. Only this Savior is God. And only this God is the Savior. Notice, for example, Hosea 13:4: "But I am the LORD your God, who brought you out of Egypt. You shall acknowledge no God but me, no Savior except me."

This Lord who rescued Israel from bondage is the only one that the Israelites were to acknowledge as God, and the only one that they were to acknowledge as Savior. Their faith was monotheistic, or supportive of faith in only one God who alone saves. In other words, they were expected to assume that *only God can save*. When it comes to salvation, there is no other choice but this God who delivered Israel from bondage in Egypt. It is either this God or spiritual death.

Notice that the entire verse assumes that the terms *God* and *Savior* are interchangeable and mutually defining. If only the Lord of the exodus is to be acknowledged as God, then only this Lord is to be acknowledged as the Savior, as well. If the Israelites were to have only this Lord as God, they were to have only this Lord as Savior. The two terms *God* and *Savior* are inseparable, overlapping in meaning, and mutually defining. An essential part of what it means to be God is the capacity to save. The one God who rescued the Israelites is the only God, which means also that this God is the only Savior.

At this point someone might object that the Israelites were to acknowledge only the Lord of the exodus as *their* God and Savior. Perhaps there were other gods or other paths to salvation besides the God of the exodus, but for various reasons the Israelites were to recognize only their liberator as their God and Savior. But the Old Testament also notes clearly that there is no other God but the Lord of the exodus and no other Savior but this God. If we turn to Isaiah 45 we find God saying, "I am the LORD, and there is no other; apart from me there is no God" (v. 5). And again, "Surely God is with you, and there is no other; there is no other God" (v. 14). Only this God is God. Only this God is the Creator (v. 18). Only this God can save.

Note Isaiah 45:20–24:

> "Gather together and come;
>> assemble, you fugitives from the nations.
>> Ignorant are those who carry about idols of wood,
>> who pray to gods that cannot save.
> Declare what is to be, present it—
>> let them take counsel together.
>> Who foretold this long ago,
>> who declared it from the distant past?

> Was it not I, the LORD?
> And there is no God apart from me,
>   a righteous God and a Savior;
>   there is none but me.
> "Turn to me and be saved,
>   all you ends of the earth;
>   for I am God, and there is no other.
> By myself I have sworn,
>   my mouth has uttered in all integrity
>   a word that will not be revoked:
>   Before me every knee will bow;
>   by me every tongue will swear.
> They will say of me, 'In the LORD alone
>   are righteousness and strength.'"
>   All who have raged against him
>   will come to him and be put to shame.

The other gods cannot save, for only the God of the exodus is righteousness and strength: "Ignorant are those who carry about idols of wood, who pray to gods that cannot save" (v. 20).

The Old Testament is also clear that salvation cannot come from self-reliance or by trusting in others to save. Only the Lord is the Savior, the rock, the refuge, and the shield (2 Samuel 22:3). God saves even from death itself (Psalm 68:20). Death reveals the failure of mere mortal humanity to save itself, which is why we are not to trust in mere humans to save us (Psalm 146:2–4). Indeed, "Israel will be saved by the LORD with an everlasting salvation; you will never be put to shame or disgraced, to ages everlasting" (Isaiah 45:17). Only the eternal God revives and restores; the divine face or presence shines on us, bringing salvation (Psalm 80:18–19). We all grow weary and fail but the everlasting Lord and Creator shall never grow faint. Only those who trust in God will be saved. Notice the words of Isaiah again (Isaiah 40:28–31):

> Do you not know?
>> Have you not heard?
>> The Lord is the everlasting God,
>> the Creator of the ends of the earth.
>> He will not grow tired or weary,
>> and his understanding no one can fathom.
> He gives strength to the weary
>> and increases the power of the weak.
> Even youths grow tired and weary,
>> and young men stumble and fall;
> but those who hope in the Lord
>> will renew their strength.
>> They will soar on wings like eagles;
>> they will run and not grow weary,
>> they will walk and not be faint.

When it comes to salvation, God is indeed the only choice available. All creatures fail; only God can endure as the rock of eternal salvation. Hope in anyone else besides God is based on sinking sand. Indeed, God said: "Turn to me and be saved, all you ends of the earth; for I am God, and there is no other" (Isaiah 45:22).

Someone may ask at this point, "But doesn't the Old Testament assume that people can save themselves by following the law of God?" Not so. I'm surprised how often I hear from students the idea that salvation comes by following the law according to the Old Testament. I often wonder where this idea comes from, since it is nowhere stated in the Bible. The Bible is clear that the sacrifices mandated in the law could not remove sin (Hebrews 10:4) and that no commandment can give life (Romans 8:3; Galatians 3:21). The law was meant to witness to the flourishing or renewal of life and even to lead to this life. The Old Testament promised a truly blessed life to those who lived according to the law. Note Deuteronomy 30:16: "For I command you today to love the LORD your God, to walk in his ways, and to keep his commands, decrees and laws; then you will live and increase, and the LORD your God will bless you in the land you are entering to possess." The law alone, however, could not deliver on this promise of the blessed life because we are not able in our own strength to meet the law's demands and the law is not able to save us. The law required God's liberating act and the gift of God's Spirit to result in the blessed life promised to those who live by it.

The law played a vital role in the life of Israel, but the Old Testament is clear that *only* God is to be acknowledged as the Savior and Redeemer. The giving of the law was prefaced by the dramatic event of the exodus, God's chief act of redeeming Israel by grace. Exodus 20:1–3 states, "And God spoke all these words: 'I am the LORD your God, who brought you out of Egypt, out of the land of slavery. You shall have no other gods before me.'" The other commandments follow this verse in sequential order. In other words, this text in which the law is given places God's role as Redeemer and Deliverer *first,* and the challenge for Israel to obey God's commands then follows in *second place.* The implication is that liberating grace comes first and obedience second (dependent on it).

This order in Exodus 20:1–3 is important. The commandments come second and not first. God did not say to Moses before the exodus occurred, "Here are the commandments. When the Israelites have sufficiently obeyed these laws, I will save them." No! God called them and saved them by grace first. God became their Lord and delivered them before giving them the commandments. All they had to do was to trust in God's promise, just like Abraham trusted in God's promises and was reckoned as righteous because of it (Genesis 15:6). Though adherence to the law was vital to Israel's faithfulness in the Old Testament, ultimately Israel was righteous by taking refuge in God and placing trust and hope in him (Psalm 5:12; 14:5; 31:18; 33:1; 36:10; 52:6; 94:15, 21; 118:15, 20). God gave the Israelites the commands only *after* the deliverance of the exodus so that they could live out that salvation in a way consistent with the freedom that it brought. Moreover, Ezekiel 36:27 adds that the gift of new life through the Holy Spirit will provide the means by which the law and its blessings can be had among those who are redeemed by God.

In fact, the whole purpose of the law was to remind the Israelites that only God is the Deliverer and to keep them acknowledging the Lord alone as the source of all salvation and blessing. Deuteronomy 8:10–18 is clear in this regard. I will quote the entire text, for it is worth reading in full:

> When you have eaten and are satisfied, praise the LORD your God for the good land he has given you. Be careful that you do not forget the LORD your God, failing to observe his commands, his laws and his decrees that I am giving you this day. Otherwise, when you eat and are satisfied, when you build fine houses and settle down, and when your herds and flocks grow large and your silver and gold increase and all you have is multiplied, then your heart will become proud and you will forget the LORD your God, who brought you out of Egypt, out of the land of slavery. He led you through the vast and dreadful desert, that thirsty and waterless land, with its venomous snakes and scorpions. He brought you water out of hard rock. He gave you manna to eat in the desert, something

your fathers had never known, to humble and to test you so that in the end it might go well with you. You may say to yourself, "My power and the strength of my hands have produced this wealth for me." But remember the LORD your God, for it is he who gives you the ability to produce wealth, and so confirms his covenant, which he swore to your forefathers, as it is today.

Notice that obedience to the commandments was to be the means by which Israel remembered and recognized God alone as the source of all blessing. Neglecting the law might deceive the people into thinking that the blessings were gained by their own hand. Any assumption that obedience to the law could save contradicted the very meaning implied by the commandments of God.

Interestingly, Jesus never scolded the Jewish leaders for wanting to obey God's commandments (cf. Matthew 5:19), only for trivializing the law by focusing on purity rituals or other ceremonies and forgetting the weighty matters of love and justice (Matthew 23:23). Paul agreed concerning God's moral commands, "Circumcision is nothing and uncircumcision is nothing. Keeping God's commands is what counts" (1 Corinthians 7:19). Of course, both Jesus and Paul condemned any illusion that salvation comes in any other way than by the grace and mercy of God (Luke 18:11–14; Ephesians 2:8).

Acknowledging the Lord as the source of all blessing is a form of devotion to God. So the chief law is to love the Lord with our entire being, which is why the commandments are to be written on the heart (Deuteronomy 6:4–6). The law was meant as a means by which the abundant life given as a gift is affirmed and lived out. The law is not far but near, in the heart and the mouth (Deuteronomy 30:6, 11–14). The prophets looked forward to the day when God would give the divine Spirit within in order to move people to obey (Ezekiel 36:27).

God's gracious presence to redeem is always the beginning, the essence, and the end of obedience to the commandments.

The New Testament does not part from this fundamental principle that only God can save, except Christ looms large as the fulfillment of the law and the means by which God ultimately saves humanity. Revelation 7:10 has the heavenly voices cry out, "Salvation belongs to our God." Salvation belongs to God. "Salvation is found in no one else" (Acts 4:12). Saving is a divine capacity and not a creaturely one. Only the Creator can redeem and turn the corrupted creation into a new, incorruptible creation. It is only by the grace of God that we can be saved, "and this not from yourselves, it is the gift of God" (Ephesians 2:8).

God "saved us, not because of righteous things we had done, but because of his mercy" (Titus 3:5). Both salvation and judgment are in God's hands alone. Indeed, "there is only one Lawgiver and Judge, the one who is able to save and destroy" (James 4:12). In addition to acknowledging the Lord, the law reveals God's righteous standards and shows us our failings and our need of a Savior (Romans 7:11–14). It also helps to guide the new life given by grace and lived by trusting in God for salvation. The righteous, however, will live fundamentally by faith in God to save (Romans 1:17). The New Testament is in agreement with the Old that only God can save. The gospel of Jesus Christ fulfills the "gospel" implied in the law given to Moses. It is for this reason that the late Czech theologian Jan Milič Lochman referred to the law of Moses as the "other form of the gospel." The law bears witness to the flourishing or renewal of life as does the gospel or good news of Jesus Christ, except the gospel of Christ comes first, since it alone grants the salvation and freedom that the law assumes but cannot give to us.

This fundamental premise in the Bible that salvation belongs only to God leads to other themes as well. We trust and hope only in God for salvation (Isaiah 40:31); we glorify and worship only God (Romans 1:21–22; Revelation 22:8–9); we seek to place only God first and above all else. We do these things because we acknowledge only God as the one who can save and does save. To trust or hope in any other being or object, to glorify or worship anyone or anything else, to place anyone or anything else above God or on the same level as God means idolatry and bondage, the very opposite of salvation. There is no possibility of acknowledging any other Savior besides God. There is no possibility of compromise regarding salvation. Only the God revealed in Scripture as the God of the exodus and as the God of Jesus Christ can save. There is no other God; there is no other Savior. In the Bible, the choices are only two: God or destruction. Let us look briefly at why the Bible regards any attempt to deny this principle as idolatry.

The Danger of Idolatry

According to the Scriptures, we commit idolatry if we deny that only God can save. This is because, as we noted above, salvation belongs to God alone. To trust in anyone or anything else for salvation is to place this thing on the same level as God (or even above God). But God is jealous for our devotion and will not tolerate any competition. We glorify and worship only God for only God is the Creator and Redeemer. Idols are not to be trusted in for salvation or worshiped "for I, the LORD your God, am a jealous God" (Exodus 20:5).

What exactly is idolatry? On one level, the sin of idolatry seems simple. We are not to make any images as objects of worship. Exodus 20:3–5 is clear: "You shall have no other gods before me. You shall not make for yourself an idol in the form of anything in heaven above or on the earth beneath or in the waters below. You shall not bow down to them or worship them."

Paul even went so far as to indicate that idolatry is at the root of humanity's rebellion against God, noting that God gave humanity over to their sinful desires because they chose not to glorify God but glorified the images that they created instead. Note Romans 1:21–23: "For although they knew God, they neither glorified him as God nor gave thanks to him, but their thinking became futile and their foolish hearts were darkened. Although they claimed to be wise, they became fools and exchanged the glory of the immortal God for images made to look like mortal man and birds and animals and reptiles."

Why did people make idols in the first place? The reason is worth exploring. It is important to note what the ancients attempted to do with idols. "Gods" (so called) could seem so distant and unpredictable. The temptation for those devoted to them was to find a way of making them "user-friendly." The goal was to figure a way of bringing the gods down into temples and homes so as to communicate with them and find ways of getting them to do whatever people desired. Idols become the means by which this could supposedly be done. Idols were a form of religious technology, for they allowed the gods to become functional within the demands of human religion.

The gods might be user-friendly, but the Lord of the universe is not. No image can capture the Lord: "To whom, then, will you compare God? What image will you compare him to?" (Isaiah 40:18). "For all the gods of the nations are idols, but the LORD made the heavens" (Psalm 96:5). There is no possibility of ranking the gods with the Lord: "Do not make any gods to be alongside me; do not make for yourselves gods of silver or gods of gold" (Exodus 20:23). God cannot be ranked with the gods of idols within temples and religions made by human hands: "The God who made the world and everything in it is the Lord of heaven and earth and does not live in temples built by hands. And he is not served by human hands, as if he needed anything, because he himself gives all men life and breath and everything else" (Acts 17:24–25).

These idols are in themselves nothing more than empty material: "They have thrown their gods into the fire and destroyed them, for they were not gods but only wood and stone, fashioned by human hands" (Isaiah 37:19). But these idols were not to be taken lightly, for they represented a certain myth of human control and power. The gods that legitimated these idols were nonexistent and powerless, to be sure. But the human lust for power that fueled the making of religious systems of idols and rituals was real. Like the inhabitants of the early city of Babel who tried to make a name for themselves by building a temple to reach heaven (Genesis 11), people used idols to impose their will on God. Paul preached to the residents of Athens that God is not an object made by human hands and subject to manipulation. We are rather made by God to do God's will: "Therefore since we are God's offspring, we should not think that the divine being is like gold or silver or stone—an image made by man's design and skill. In the past God overlooked such ignorance, but now he commands all people everywhere to repent" (Acts 17:29–30).

It is important to point out that idolatry does not just take place through the making of images and the worshiping of them. *Any* human effort to manipulate God or to glorify the creature made by God (or the creature's works) is idolatry. Any effort to bind God to an image that we create in our minds or to our own plans and schemes is idolatry. Any attempt to elevate anything other than God to the level of the absolute or to grant it limitless importance is also idolatry. Any illusion that we can save ourselves or that someone or something else can fulfill our ultimate and God-given yearnings is idolatry. There may not be physical images involved, but it is idolatry nonetheless.

According to the Scriptures, we glorify God by recognizing God *alone* as the source of all life and salvation. "The LORD is my strength and my song; he has become my salvation. He is my God, and I will praise him" (Exodus 15:2). Praising God helps us to remember God's redemptive deeds and many blessings: "Praise the LORD, O my soul, and forget not all his benefits" (Psalm 103:2). Even when our prayers are not answered as we expect, God is still praised for the bounty of grace is always sufficient for every need (2 Corinthians 12:1–10). "Praise be to the God and Father of our Lord Jesus Christ, the Father of compassion and the God of all comfort" (2 Corinthians 1:3). God alone as the rock in all situations of life is the one worthy of praise: "The LORD lives! Praise be to my Rock! Exalted be God, the Rock, my Savior" (2 Samuel 22:47). God proves faithful and worthy of praise: "Praise be to the LORD, the God of Israel, who with his hands has fulfilled what he promised with his mouth" (2 Chronicles 6:4).

God is eternal, the only one on whom we can rely in this changing world. So God is the one worthy of praise: "Stand up and praise the LORD your God, who is from everlasting to everlasting" (Nehemiah 9:5). Our praise of God leads naturally to a witness to God as Lord and Savior: "I will praise you, O LORD, with all my heart; I will tell of all your wonders" (Psalm 9:1). We praise God not only for what God does for us but for who God is in relation to us: "You are awesome, O God, in your sanctuary; the God of Israel gives power and strength to his people. Praise be to God!" (Psalm 68:35). Praise exalts God above all else, so there is no possibility of there being any competition for our praises. "I will bow down toward your holy temple and will praise your name for your love and your faithfulness, for you have exalted above all things your name and your word" (Psalm 138:2). We glorify a God whose greatness cannot be grasped: "Great is the LORD and most worthy of praise; his greatness no one can fathom" (Psalm 145:3).

God is exalted above all else, "for his name alone is exalted; his splendor is above the earth and the heavens" (Psalm 148:13). Being praised is the prerogative of God alone: "Amen! Praise and glory and wisdom and thanks and honor and power and strength be to our God for ever and ever. Amen!" (Revelation 7:12). Only God is to be worshiped (Revelation 22:8–9). Sin causes humanity to fall short of God's glory (Romans 3:23). It causes humanity to worship the work of their own hands or the idols rather than God (Romans 1:21–23). But we are reconciled to God through Christ and with one another so that we may bring praise to God: "Accept one another, then, just as Christ accepted you, in order to bring praise to God" (Romans 15:7). Christ becomes the means by which we continuously praise God in all that we do: "Through Jesus, therefore, let us continually offer to God a sacrifice of praise—the fruit of lips that confess his name" (Hebrews 13:15).

In short, not only is God alone the Savior, but any denial of this fact is described in the Bible as idolatry. Since only God can save, only God is worthy to be glorified and praised. Only God is worthy to receive our ultimate trust and allegiance. Only God is to be looked on as our ultimate hope. Only God can be called absolute or of ultimate importance to life. If there were other possible saviors, then there would be other possible gods, other possible objects of our ultimate trust, hope, and allegiance.

But the Bible will not allow for this as a possibility. The world of biblical revelation assumes only *one* Lord and God who creates and redeems. There is no pantheon of gods in the Bible, so that we can attempt running to another if the god before us does not respond as expected. Only the one Creator and Redeemer revealed in the exodus can save, according to the Old Testament. The heart of true religion is to love this God with the entire heart, soul, mind, and strength and to allow for no competition for our devotion and loyalty. "Hear, O Israel: The LORD our God, the LORD is one. Love the LORD your God with all your heart and with all your soul and with all your strength" (Deuteronomy 6:4–5). This is the most important issue in our relationship with God.

The Battle for Allegiance

When I was twelve, I formed the idea that salvation was basically in my own hands. I'm sure that this was not an idea given to me by my father, for he always preached God's love and forgiveness. I'm not sure where I got it from, but there was a brief period in my early teens when this salvation-by-works idea became fixed in my mind. I had a regular routine. I would dedicate my life to God on Sunday and then feel as though I had lost my salvation on Monday, due to some type of behavior that I considered unbiblical. I would then struggle through the week not really sure of my status before God, only to rededicate myself on Sunday all over again.

On top of everything, I would attend a Christian teen camp every July in which I would repeat my weekly routine. I would spend the bulk of the week breaking every rule that I thought I could get away with only to make a firm commitment to Christ near the end of the week, before the camp ended. I would then attend the baptismal service on the final day of the camp at the lake to be rebaptized, which I thought gave me a big advantage during my new week back at home. I was baptized several times in those early teen years.

Once home, I would listen to Christian records and read the Bible for a couple days until I managed to do something sinful enough in my estimation to cause me to fall back into disfavor with God. That was my Christian life back then: feeling as though I went in and out of God's favor, depending on how "good" I was. I saw God's grace as forgiveness and another chance at being good. Once I failed to be good, I was in trouble with God all over again. My salvation was like musical chairs; I hoped I would not be found without a chair once the music stopped and my life came to an end.

I was right to think that certain behaviors did not please God and that pleasing God was indeed a vital part of the Christian life. But I failed to realize in those years that God never stopped loving me, even when my behavior may not have been biblical. What was also lacking in my thoughts was the biblical concept of the sustaining nature of God's grace. I failed to realize that God sustained me by grace even though I made mistakes and didn't always live up to my faith. His love never let go of me. To have thought that I could save myself through good behavior was a subtle form of idolatry, one from which God had to deliver me. All Christians have some form of idolatry in their lives from which God must deliver them and is delivering them.

In fact, there is a battle going on between the biblical idea that only God can save and the delusion that we can save ourselves, or between faith and idolatry. The struggle between these proposals is enormously important and runs throughout Scripture. The book of Daniel tells us that the whole of human history can be viewed through the lens of this epic struggle. King Nebuchadnezzar asked Daniel to interpret a dream. The dream featured a statue (Daniel 2:31), which was probably a large idol. The head of gold was the Babylonian empire; the arms and chest of silver, the belly and thighs of bronze, the legs of iron, and the feet of iron mixed with clay all represented empires inferior to the Babylonian (e.g., Daniel 2:39). Scholars have debated the identities of these empires, but they most likely include the Medes and Persians, the Grecian empire, and possibly the Roman Empire (and perhaps the kingdom of Antichrist at the end of time). But the identities of the empires are not crucial to the passage, since the meaning is that they all represent the same idolatry. The idolatrous empires are weakening from within as the rulers and peoples change (the strength of the metal decreases from the head to the feet of the great idol). Yet they all make up one large idol, one massive attempt by peoples and rulers to lift themselves and their goals to be of ultimate importance. They all participate in the same idolatry.

This is Daniel's view of human history. History has its positive side, since humans never lose their identity as beings in the image of God. As Acts 17 notes, God dispersed the various peoples throughout the earth so that within their unique histories and cultures they might reach out for and perhaps find God (vv. 26–27). Yet Daniel is clear that there is also a dark side to history that resembles the tower of Babel. There is a self-determination that does not acknowledge God or recognize anything beyond the quest for power. This quest continues throughout the centuries until God's kingdom overthrows it. The kingdom of God comes at the idol as a large boulder to strike it at its base. It then crumbles and the kingdom of God reigns on the rubble (Daniel 2:44–45).

In the book of Revelation this end is described as follows:

> The seventh angel sounded his trumpet, and there were loud voices in heaven, which said:
>
> > "The kingdom of the world has become the kingdom
> >   of our Lord and of his Christ,
> >   and he will reign for ever and ever."
>
> And the twenty-four elders, who were seated on their thrones before God, fell on their faces and worshiped God, saying:
>
> > "We give thanks to you, Lord God Almighty,
> >   the One who is and who was,

because you have taken your great power
　　and have begun to reign.
The nations were angry;
　　and your wrath has come.
The time has come for judging the dead,
　　and for rewarding your servants the prophets
and your saints and those who reverence your name,
　　both small and great—
and for destroying those who destroy the earth."
(Revelation 11:15–18)

The nations are angry indeed! They have pursued self-interest in the most destructive ways. They have spurned God's reign and offer of love. As a result, the destruction that they have brought on the earth has fallen on them. The nations have been liberated from their strangle hold under the dark powers and God has begun to reign on the earth. The idols have fallen and have been revealed as demonic delusions. The Creator has taken rightful lordship over the earth and now receives the glory due only to God. God will indeed have the last word, the word that was spoken by the prophets and decisively in Jesus Christ. All of the false paths to "salvation" have closed under judgment and only God is left as the rightful Lord of life and salvation. It will be known throughout the earth that *only God can save*!

This principle of faith is the first station of our journey. If we board the train at this station, there will be no way to leave the train until we arrive at the end station called "God Is a Trinity."

Study Questions:

1. What do we say to those who make fun of the notion of salvation?

2. What does 2 Corinthians 5:1–5 tell us about what we yearn for and our inability to get it in our own power?

3. Discuss three Scripture texts that support the role of God alone as Savior.

4. Can people save themselves through obedience to the law according to the Old Testament? Explain your answer.

5. What is idolatry? Explain your answer.

6. Explain the battle for allegiance in the Old Testament.

4
STATION TWO
The Son Saves

The station called "Only God Can Save" is where we boarded the train. The next station is called "The Son Saves." How did we get from the first station to this one? Is this station on course with the first or have we taken a detour? It is my purpose here to show that this station affirms Christ's deity and is the necessary next step in our journey, for the first station won't allow there to be *any* Savior but God. If only God can save, and Jesus the Son saves, he *must* be divine. If he is not divine, he cannot be called the Savior. But the very name of Jesus means that "he will save his people from their sins" (Matthew 1:21).

This chapter centers on Jesus Christ as sent by the heavenly Father to redeem humanity from sin and death. "For God so loved the world," wrote John, "that he gave his one and only Son, that whoever believes in him shall not perish but have eternal life" (John 3:16). John 1:18 defines the God who sent the Son as the heavenly Father. The Bible focuses God's act of salvation not only on God the heavenly Father but also on Jesus Christ as God's one and only Son. The Bible even goes so far as to say that Jesus himself can be called the Savior as well.

Jesus Saves

When I was a child, there was a large painting on the front wall of the church sanctuary of a bearded Jesus with his arms wide open seeking to embrace us all. I hadn't thought in those early years how Jesus might relate to God. I just figured that they were both on the same side and that this was enough to know. I recall once one of my Sunday school teachers telling us that God had been grieved by human sin and had asked the heavenly host who was willing to go down to earth to save us. None of the angels or Old Testament saints stepped forward to accept the task. Only Jesus, God's favored Son, was willing to do it. After that lesson, I remember looking at the portrait of Jesus on the wall as I re-entered the church sanctuary and thinking that he was a brave man, braver than Moses, Elijah, and all of the angels. I just figured that Jesus was like the rest of them, only braver. Besides, the smiling figure on the wall appealed to me. He seemed like a really nice person. Why shouldn't we glorify him every Sunday? He deserved it.

It hadn't occurred to me then that our practice of worshiping Christ and trusting in him for salvation would have been utter blasphemy if Jesus had been essentially no different from any other created being. It just wasn't clear to me then that such things were to be reserved for God alone. Even placing Jesus on the highest point of the hierarchy of created beings would not have been enough to make our worship of him or trust in him for salvation any more acceptable. There is an eternal gulf between the everlasting Creator and all finite or created beings. Only the one who creates and gives life, only the one who saves, can be worshiped and trusted in for salvation. *There are no exceptions.*

As we noted in our last chapter, *only God can save*. Here in this chapter, I want to show that *Jesus saves*. The fact that Jesus is therefore divine seems like airtight logic, and it is. Only if this is the case can we justifiably worship him and trust in him for salvation. But does Jesus really save? There are verses that stress the fact that God saves *through* Jesus. God sent Jesus to be the one through whom God would save the world from sin and death (John 3:16). John wrote that "God did not send his Son into the world to condemn the world, but to save the world through him" (John 3:17).

Paul wrote that God "reconciled us to himself through Christ" (2 Corinthians 5:18). God has indeed adopted us as sons and daughters "through Jesus Christ" (Ephesians 1:5). God has also given us spiritual new birth and "made us alive with Christ even when we were dead in transgressions" (Ephesians 2:5). God has "raised us up with Christ" and seated us in heavenly places (Ephesians 2:6). The fruit of righteousness comes forth in our lives "through Jesus Christ—to the glory and praise of God" (Philippians 1:11). We are made holy by God "through the sacrifice of the body of Jesus Christ" (Hebrews 10:10).

This entire stress on God's saving us "through" or "with" Christ is important, because it shows that Jesus saves in cooperation or loving interaction with the Father and the agency of the Spirit. The Father has saved through the one and only Son and by means of the power of the Holy Spirit. Jesus did not save in isolation from the other persons of the Trinity. This insight goes into the meaning of Station Two and will become important later on when interpreting the meaning of our final destination.

But this stress on salvation *through* Jesus might lead some to wrongly believe that Jesus is not actually the Savior or Redeemer, but rather that God saves through him or through his ministry, much like God saves people through our ministries. But such a conclusion is not warranted from a thorough reading of the New Testament. God may indeed be said to save through Jesus, but the Scriptures do not hesitate to say that Jesus saves as well. Christ was given the name Jesus at birth "because he will save his people from their sins" (Matthew 1:21). John the Baptist called Jesus "the Lamb of God, who takes away the sin of the world!" (John 1:29). A mere mortal can proclaim God's forgiveness, but he or she cannot take away the sins of humanity. Only God can do that. Paul noted that "Christ Jesus came into the world to save sinners—of whom I am the worst" (1 Timothy 1:15).

According to the New Testament, Christ redeemed us (Galatians 3:13). Christ redeemed us by his blood (Revelation 5:9). Christ is the Savior who destroyed death and brought life (2 Timothy 1:10). What mere human can destroy death and bring new life? Not only did God raise Jesus from the dead (Romans 8:11) but Jesus said that he would raise himself as well (John 2:19–20). What mere mortal can raise himself or herself from the dead?

Christ is freely called the Savior in the New Testament (Acts 13:23; 2 Timothy 1:10; Titus 1:4, 2:13, 3:6; 2 Peter 1:11, 2:20, 3:18). Obviously, the New Testament is not using the term *Savior* in regard to Jesus to merely depict someone who helps us in life or who points the way to God. Something much deeper is in view, since Jesus is said to have saved in a way that is applicable only to God. Jesus cancelled sin and destroyed death and breathed forth the Spirit to give new life (John 20:22). Jesus assumed the authority to forgive sins even before his death and resurrection, an authority that belongs to God alone (Mark 2:5–7). Jesus saved not just by drawing attention to God *but by assuming the right and power to save.* He also claimed to be the resurrection and the life so that those who live forever do so by believing in him (John 11:25). He told his disciples, "Trust in God, trust also in me" (John 14:1), as though he deserves the same trust as the Father for salvation. The conclusion is clear: not only does God save *through* Jesus, *Jesus saves* as well. In other words, God saves through

Jesus in that Jesus himself also assumes the role of Savior. Sharing in the Father's deity, Jesus is able to participate fully in saving humanity.

How does Jesus save? This is a difficult question that has occupied theologians and church leaders for centuries. The New Testament uses a variety of descriptions and metaphors for describing how Jesus saves. We can only scratch the surface here. It all starts with the fact that the eternal Son of God came to earth and was born as a flesh-and-blood human being, Jesus of Nazareth. This is what theologians call the incarnation. John tells us that the Word (or self-expression) of God the only Son "became flesh" and dwelt among us (John 1:14). The idea here is that the Son of God, who was the revelation or self-expression of the heavenly Father (see John 1:18), took up his dwelling among us in the "tent" of human flesh.

When gazing on the face of Jesus, a person looked at the very Son of God. He left the glories of deity to empty himself and make himself "nothing" for us. Not that he gave up his deity (he couldn't do that), but he left the glories of his deity at the right hand of the Father to descend into human flesh. He descended into the depths of life in human flesh, even to the point of dying a criminal's death on the cross, to save us. That ancient hymn that Paul quoted in Philippians 2 tells the story:

> Who, being in very nature God,
>> did not consider equality with God something
>>> to be grasped,
> but made himself nothing,
>> taking the very nature of a servant,
>> being made in human likeness.
> And being found in appearance as a man,
>> he humbled himself
>> and became obedient to death—
>>> even death on a cross!

> Therefore God exalted him to the highest place
>> and gave him the name that is above every name,
> that at the name of Jesus every knee should bow,
>> in heaven and on earth and under the earth,
> and every tongue confess that Jesus Christ is Lord,
>> to the glory of God the Father.

While on earth Jesus did not grasp after equality with God in public so as to gain recognition from others. He was already divine in nature. This is not why he became flesh. He became flesh to identify with the lowly and to join the despised.

Why did Jesus descend into the depths of human flesh? The implication of the New Testament is that the Son became human so as to "taste death" for us. Jesus is said to have tasted death for us so as to defeat death and the forces of darkness through his resurrection (Colossians 1:13; Hebrews 2:14–15). As flesh, he was also able to bear the curse of sin for us so that we could be free from its guilt and power (Galatians 3:13–14; 1 Peter 2:24). He was our substitute, paying a debt that we couldn't pay in order to reconcile us to God. By becoming flesh, he was also able to show us who God is in a way that we could understand (John 1:1–14). The Bible tells us that his love is so great for us that he became one of us to set us free. He entered into our shameful existence and experienced it with us as the means of liberating us and leading us out. In this way, Jesus bound himself to us in saving us so that we might be bound to him in love by accepting him.

John stated it this way: "This is how God showed his love among us: He sent his one and only Son into the world that we might live through him. This is love: not that we loved God, but that he loved us and sent his Son as an atoning sacrifice for our sins" (1 John 4:9–10). In becoming human, God wasn't compelled by any cosmic law to which he must bow a knee. God is sovereign and is bound by no law except the law of divine love, God's very nature. God's love compelled Jesus to become flesh and to save us from within the darkness of our captivity.

Jesus was like the shepherd who goes into the thorn bushes to save the lost, entangled sheep, or the widow who searches the floor of her hut for the lost coin (Luke 15). By sending Jesus into the world, God followed us down the twisted path of our disobedience and met us at our lowest point in order to free us and to bring us out. In the process, God took on our shame and suffering in order to give us the blessing of immortal life with him. The goal was to convert us by divine love.

Let's explore still more deeply how Jesus' death and resurrection saved us. The Bible talks about Christ's death as a "ransom" (Mark 10:45), meaning that Jesus came into the enemy camp and did what was necessary to deliver us from captivity and to win us back to God. The idea of "redemption" (e.g., Galatians 3:14), or setting captives free by paying a debt that is owed, is similar in meaning. The Bible does not elaborate on the particulars of how this ransom or redemption was won by Christ on the cross and in the resurrection. Speculations about a payment made to the devil to set us free from darkness were rejected long ago, since the devil deceived humanity and has no legitimate claim to any payments. God does not owe the devil anything but judgment!

A payment may be said to be made to God in the sense that Christ fulfilled all righteousness on behalf of humanity before God. But caution must be exercised here so as not to lose sight of the fact that God the Father sent the Son to the earth to ransom humanity to begin with. The Father was not a passive judge who needed to be persuaded to forgive humanity by the payment of the Son! The Father and the Son were of one mind and both participated in the mission of the Son to find lost humanity. God is the one who seeks the lost (Luke

15). Perhaps it is best not to speculate too much on how or to whom Jesus made "payment" in order to ransom or redeem humanity from sin and death. The New Testament simply stresses that Jesus came into our situation of sin, sorrow, and death to set us free and to bring us back home to God.

The Bible also uses the metaphor of "sacrifice" in order to explain how Jesus' death was "atoning" or reconciling. Hebrews 10 notes that the sacrificial system as part of Jewish law in the Old Testament times was only a "shadow" of the redemption that Christ would come to bring. It was not so much that sacrifice was required to redeem us but the fulfillment of the Father's will (Hebrews 10:1–10). Sacrifices in the Old Testament times as a shadow of the coming redemption could not themselves redeem. Israelites at that time were saved by hoping in God and by looking forward to the coming day of redemption. The sacrifices symbolized the fact that sin has innocent victims and that God would one day transfer the sin of the people to the ultimate innocent lamb (who would be Jesus). By hoping in God through these sacrifices, God allowed the Israelites to be counted righteous already, even before Jesus' redemptive work on the cross. They were able to draw from the power of that event even before it happened. In other words, the sacrificial system was the shadow cast backwards in time by the cross.

Sacrifices were part of the Jewish temple cult. They were also a form of worship of God. As the ultimate sacrifice, Jesus was the living temple of the Spirit dedicated to God and willing to carry away the sins of the world. He descended into that state of darkness and separation from God that we occupy. But in doing so, he was still the temple of God empowered by the divine Spirit (Hebrews 9:14). He experienced our alienation from God, even crying out, "My God, my God, why have you forsaken me?" (Mark 15:34). But God had not ultimately forsaken him. The Spirit's presence was hidden beneath the suffering and darkness that the Son bore for us. And in three days, the Father raised the Son from the dead by the Spirit, not abandoning him to the grave (Acts 2:27; Romans 1:4). Jesus as the divine Son and the temple of God's presence descended into our alienation and abandonment in order to reconcile us to God's presence and restore us to our purpose as dwelling places of God's Spirit.

Ultimately, Jesus imparts God's Holy Spirit to us so that we can share in Jesus' sonship and commune with his heavenly Father (Romans 8:15–16). In general, Jesus engaged in a "blessed exchange" with us. He took on our flesh, our sin, our death in order that we could be reconciled to God and take from him God's eternal life in the form of the gift of the Spirit. Jesus imparts God's Spirit to us as the means by which we can partake of the victory that he won for us by becoming flesh and by dying and rising again (Acts 2:32–33). The Spirit leads us to Christ and then binds us to Christ once we accept him as our Savior and dedicate ourselves to him through faith. The Spirit within is the seal that solidifies our relationship with Christ and guarantees the full reception of salvation that is yet to come in the resurrection of the dead (Ephesians 1:13–14; Romans 8:11).

Jesus Is Divine

I stood there with my church's youth group after an afternoon of hanging out together. I was a college student involved in summer ministry and anxious to teach the youth all that I knew about the Bible. At that time, it was popular to call Jesus the "Bridge Over Troubled Water" due to the fact that Simon and Garfunkel had just had a major hit song by that title. So I decided to give the kids a Bible study with that as the title: "Jesus Is the Bridge Over Troubled Water." He is the bridge to God. I pretended to be God (!) and the kids stood apart from me as symbolic of humanity.

Then I asked them, "Who among you has the power to defeat sin and death and to rescue humanity? Who has the power to reconcile humanity to God?" They stood there looking at each other with big smiles and nervous looks. I stood there waiting patiently for one of them to step forward, but no one had the nerve. Finally, one of them asked, "Are you kidding?" Then I asked, "Who has the power over life and death? Who has the power over sin?" No sooner had I asked when a young girl said loudly, "Jesus!" as though answering a question on a quiz show. "That's right," I said. "Jesus is the bridge over troubled water!"

So true. Yet I thought about that lesson years later, and I realized that there was a missing step in that little drama that I did with the kids as a youth leader. When asking them who had the power over sin and death, I should have led them *first* to say "God!" Indeed, it is "God who gives life to the dead and calls things that are not as though they were" (Romans 4:17). Only God has this power, for only God as the Creator can give life or renew it. I have since then become fond of telling my students that since God is the only one who can defeat sin and death and give new life, God must be the bridge to God's self. There can be no bridge to God other than God! My common saying has become "The only way *to* God is *through* God." God is the only means of reaching God.

With that as a middle step, we can understand the significance of saying that Jesus is the bridge to God. His role as the bridge over troubled water is not only due to his being human (as our representative). If Jesus were merely human (or merely a creature created by God) he could not defeat sin and death and reconcile us to God. Jesus had to be divine to do that. His humanity was his point of contact with us, and his deity gave him the capacity to save us. Jesus had to be divine to be the bridge to God, because the only way to God is through God.

Let's continue to keep in mind that only God can save (Hosea 13:4). Because Jesus saves, just like God saves, Jesus must also be regarded as divine. So Jesus is worshiped in the New Testament with the *same praise* that is directed to God the Father. Revelation 5 is a case in point. We notice in this chapter that the heavenly hosts regard Christ as redeeming us and making us a kingdom of priests to God (Revelation 5:9–10). Jesus did not just proclaim redemption or the kingdom, he redeemed us and made us a kingdom. In the very next verses these hosts proclaim that Jesus is worthy "to receive power and wealth and wisdom and strength and honor and glory and praise!" (5:12).

That this praise is exactly the same worship granted to God is shown in verse 13: "Then I heard every creature in heaven and on earth and under the earth and on the sea, and all that is in them, singing: 'To him who sits on the throne and to the Lamb be praise and honor and glory and power, for ever and ever!'" The same praise directed to the God who sits on the throne is directed also to the Lamb, Jesus Christ. The logic of Revelation 5 is as follows: if Christ does what only God can do (redeem), then Christ receives what only God can receive (worship). The inescapable conclusion is that Christ is divine.

John, the author of Revelation, was not recording this to make the point that beings other than God can receive the same worship as God. John knew that such a practice would be idolatry or blasphemy. When John fell before an angel to worship him, the angel stated firmly, "Do not do it! I am a fellow servant with you and with your brothers the prophets and of all who keep the words of this book. Worship God!" (Revelation 22:9). If only God is to receive worship in Revelation, and not the servants of God, why then does Revelation have the heavenly hosts worship Christ in chapter 5? The reason is that Christ is divine. John makes both God the Father and Jesus eternal (the First and the

Last, Revelation 1:8, 17). The only conclusion is that Revelation treats Jesus as God, meaning that Jesus *is* divine.

This scriptural logic runs throughout the Bible. Even in the Old Testament, the Son of Man (or Messiah) who will deliver his people and be given authority to reign over God's kingdom will be worshiped along with God (Daniel 7:14). Jesus in John's Gospel is the Lamb that takes away the sins of the world (John 1:29). He is the light that saves those who believe in him (1:3–13); he is the divine life that saves, as well (11:25). He is the way, the truth, and the life that we must receive to be saved (14:6). He did not just point the way to God; he *is* the way to God (remember, the only way to God is through God). He did not just speak the truth; he *is* the truth. He did not just offer new life; he *is* that life, the very life of God who saves.

Jesus even breathed forth the Spirit, the very Holy Spirit of God, so as to bring the disciples into the blessing of salvation within the new covenant (John 20:22). Only God can breathe forth the Holy Spirit (Genesis 2:7). Yet the Spirit was breathed forth by Jesus, too. No wonder Thomas then said to Christ, "My Lord and my God!" (John 20:28). If Jesus did what only God can do (save or give new life), Jesus must be recognized as God. This conclusion brings to fulfillment what is stated at the beginning of John's Gospel, where it notes that the "Word" (the person of the Son of God) was at the beginning "with God, and the Word was God" (John 1:1).

In addition, Titus 3:4 and 2 Peter 1:1 both refer to Jesus as our "God and Savior." These two terms are inseparable and mutually defining, because the Savior is automatically God and God is automatically the Savior. If Jesus is one of those, he is automatically the other by definition. I often smile when I read that there are those who try grammatically to separate the terms *God* and *Savior* in these texts, as though these were two separate beings (so as to avoid calling Jesus divine). But this separation of *God* from *Savior*, though also grammatically unlikely, is theologically impossible according to the Scripture. The Bible is clear that only God can save. If Jesus is called the *Savior*, he must also be called *God*. In fact, *Jesus* and *God* become interchangeable terms throughout the New Testament.

Jesus and *God* as Interchangeable

It is quite remarkable how the terms *Jesus* and *God* become interchangeable in the New Testament. For example, the Holy Spirit is called the "Spirit of God" in the Bible (e.g., Matthew 3:16). God said in Joel, "I will pour out my Spirit" in the latter days (Joel 2:28; see Acts 2:17). God calls the Holy Spirit "my Spirit" because the Spirit belongs uniquely to God as representative of God's presence. God breathes forth the Spirit as his very own breath (Genesis 2:7). Yet in the New Testament, the Holy Spirit is also called the Spirit of Christ (e.g., Philippians 1:19), and Christ breathed forth the Holy Spirit as his own breath (John 20:22). The Spirit belongs to Christ in the same way that the Spirit belongs to God, equating Jesus with God.

Romans 8:9 refers to the Holy Spirit as both the Spirit of God and the Spirit of Christ. The Spirit therefore belongs to Christ as much as to God. The Spirit proceeds from God the Father and is also sent by Christ (John 15:26). God will pour out the Spirit according to Joel 2:28, and Jesus pours forth the Spirit, as well (Acts 2:33). Jesus does so from the right hand of God, a position of divine authority. With regard to the Holy Spirit, *God* and *Christ* are interchangeable terms. The Spirit is breathed by both and poured forth by both. The Spirit testifies for both (John 15:26). The Spirit essentially belongs to both. The implication is that Jesus shares deity with God the Father.

The same can be said for a number of other terms. The kingdom or reign of God (e.g., Matthew 12:28) is also at the same time the kingdom or reign of Christ (e.g., Ephesians 5:5). The church of God

(Acts 20:28) is at the same time the church of Christ (Romans 16:16). The gospel of God (Romans 1:1) is also the gospel of Christ (Romans 15:19). The word of God (1 John 2:14) is also the word of Christ (Colossians 3:16). The grace of God (1 Corinthians 15:10) is also the grace of Christ (2 Corinthians 13:14). And there are many other examples. All of those designations that belong solely and uniquely to God belong also to Christ, and Christ functions in a way that is interchangeable with God. If Jesus were not divine by nature, we would have to conclude that the New Testament has confused him with God and has engaged in a subtle and dangerous form of idolatry.

This is especially true when considering the fact that Jesus encouraged his disciples to exercise the same faith in him that they exercised towards God: "Trust in God, trust also in me" (John 14:1). We trust only in God for salvation. As the Psalmist wrote concerning God, "Trust in him at all times, O people; pour out your hearts to him, for God is our refuge" (Psalms 62:8). As Peter wrote, "Your faith and hope are in God" (1 Peter 1:21). Yet the New Testament is filled with references to also having faith in Christ for salvation (Romans 3:22, 26; Galatians 2:16; 3:22, 26; 2 Timothy 3:15).

Similarly, if only God can save, then the way to salvation must be God. Remember, the only way to God is through God. If only God can save, then God must be the means of salvation in God. All of these facts point also to the fact that Jesus is identifiable with God. Jesus is divine, the great "God and Savior" (Titus 2:13; 2 Peter 1:1).

In the New Testament, believers are baptized into Christ to become members of his body (1 Corinthians 12:13). The implication is clear: to be incorporated into Christ is to be incorporated into God. We partake of Christ when we take the Lord's Supper, with the clear knowledge that in Christ we find salvation (John 6:57). To be "in Christ" is also equated in the New Testament with being "in the

Holy Spirit." These are further examples of how *Christ* and *God* are interchangeable in the New Testament.

Yet the Son is not the Father or the Holy Spirit. These persons have their unique functions, which are not to be confused. For example, the Father sent the Son (John 15:26) so that the Son could reveal the Father by becoming flesh (John 1:1–14), but the Father is never said to have been sent into the world or to have become flesh; neither is the Holy Spirit said to have become flesh, though the Spirit anoints or indwells flesh in Christ. *Christ* is seen as interchangeable with *God*, but he has a unique function in cooperation with, but also distinct from the Father and the Spirit. In general, Jesus is spoken of as the incarnation of the preeminent Son or Word of the Father.

The Preeminent Son

Imagine a church service in which people are singing songs of praise to a well-known minister like Billy Graham, or praying to him, trusting in him as their savior, calling him "Lord," vowing obedience to him, or taking the bread and the juice at the Lord's Supper in order to partake of his flesh and blood. As Graham himself would be the first to say, "Perish the thought!" Why would Christians be repulsed by this thought? Why would Graham or any other Christian leader be disgusted by the idea of having Christians relate to them in this way? Is the reason merely emotional or cultural? Or is there an actual theological reason for this negative response that has a foundation in Scripture? The latter is certainly the case. Though Christ was human and ranked himself as our representative, identifying with us before God, he was also divine, to be ranked with God. This is why we desire to worship him, trust in him for salvation, obey him as our Lord, and take the Lord's Supper in his honor. Another way of saying this is that

Jesus is the Son of God, who has preeminence among humans to be worshiped by them as Lord.

Jesus is preeminent among humans, which means that he is superior to all other servants of God and is in fact the one to whom they all point. Prophets proclaimed God's Word under the inspiration of the Holy Spirit. Elijah, Isaiah, Jeremiah, Ezekiel, Amos, and John the Baptist are among the names that come to mind when thinking of prominent prophets that preceded Christ. The Bible tells us that such prophets "spoke from God as they were carried along by the Holy Spirit" (2 Peter 1:21). Jesus was a prophet, too, but a unique one. He was also the *Son of God* (Hebrews 1:1–3).

This difference is extremely important. John the Baptist was a prophet, but he made it crystal clear that his job was only to point to the coming Christ. In fact, Christ would be so superior to him that he would not be worthy to carry Christ's sandals (Matthew 3:11). The Gospel of John tells us that the difference between John the Baptist and Jesus was the difference between the one who was sent to bear witness to the light and the light itself (John 1:6–9). The light was Christ, which everyone must receive to be born from above (John 1:10–13).

Christ is utterly unique among the prophets because he is also the Son of God (John 1:18). This Son is also called the "Word" of God the Father, because he was earmarked from all eternity to reveal the Father (1:1, 18). The prophets proclaimed the Word of God but Jesus *was* that Word. He existed "in the beginning" (1:1–2, which means "from eternity") with God the Father and even participated with the Father in creating all that there is (1:3). He created with the Father and gave life with the Father (1:3–4), so it is little wonder that he is called God, along with the Father.

John 1:1 says, "In the beginning was the Word, and the Word was with God, and the Word was God." An even better translation would be, "From all eternity was the Word, and the Word was with God, and what God was the Word was." All that God the Father was, the Father's Word, or Son, was. This is why the Son alone could reveal the Father (John 1:18). The Word came into the world (1:10), or was made flesh (1:14), in the human body of Jesus in order to be the salvation of humankind.

Hebrews 1 says something similar, telling us that prior to Christ "God spoke to our forefathers through the prophets at many times and in various ways, but in these last days he has spoken to us by his Son, whom he appointed heir of all things, and through whom he made the universe" (Hebrews 1:1–2). As in John 1, notice that the Son in Hebrews 1 existed prior to his human birth. He participated with the Father in the creation. The next verse also says that the Son sustains all things by his powerful word (Hebrews 1:3). No wonder that Hebrews should also maintain that the Son has the same nature as God, noting that "the Son is the radiance of God's glory and the exact representation of his being" (1:3). As the Father is the light, so the Son is the rays that shoot forth from this light. He is the "radiance of God's glory."

Glory belongs to God alone, but it belongs to Christ by nature, too. Jesus prayed that the Father would restore to him the glory that he had shared with the Father before the worlds were made (John 17:5). Christ is the exact representation of God's being because he shares God's nature. This is why he could do things that only God can do, such as to create and uphold the creation by his powerful word (Hebrews 1:3). There may have been many prophets, but there was only one Christ, the divine Son of the Father.

That the divine Son of God existed prior to his human birth is to be expected. The divine Son cannot have a beginning. God is by nature eternal, not having any beginning or end. My daughters, Desiree and Jasmine, have asked me more than once, "Who made

God?" My answer is always the same: "No one made God. God has no beginning, because whoever could 'make' God would then be God, and a god that could be made would be no god at all." They just stare at me in disbelief and laugh. I cannot blame them because the answer I give them is hard for our finite and limited minds to grasp.

Jesus said that the Father had loved him before the creation of the world took place, meaning before time itself began as we know it (John 17:24). Before the world and time began, Jesus shared divine glory with the Father (John 17:5). The Son had no beginning, for God has no beginning. Like the heavenly Father, the Son *is* the beginning for all else, the "First and the Last," the beginning and the end (compare Revelation 1:8 and 1:18). Time does not limit him in any way or represent his boundaries. With the divine Father, the divine Son is the boundary for all else, including time. He does not have a beginning or an end; he *is* the beginning and the end (*telos*, or ultimate purpose) for all else. He is the First and the Last (Revelation 1:17).

Jesus pointed to his own eternal nature as divine when he said, "Before Abraham was born, I am!" (John 8:58). Abraham was a major figure in Old Testament times, born at least two thousand years before Christ. Yet before Abraham *was,* Christ *is*; in other words, Christ existed beyond the limits of time and space as we know it. Interestingly, God is called "the Alpha and the Omega" in Revelation 1:8, which means "the first and the last," because *alpha* and *omega* are the first and last letters of the Greek alphabet. Calling God the first and the last (the beginning and the end) means that God is eternal, having no beginning or end, but being that beginning and end for all else. Christ is also called "the First and the Last" in Revelation 1:17. Christ shares eternity with the Father because Christ, too, is divine.

As the preeminent Son, Christ is called the "firstborn" of all creation in Colossians 1:15. Of course, the firstborn Son in ancient biblical culture (as in many cultures today) inherits and is the favored child. Christ is the firstborn Son of the heavenly Father not because he had a beginning in time, but rather because he inherits all the glory that belongs to the heavenly Father. When we move down three verses to Colossians 1:18, we find that Christ is also called the "firstborn from among the dead," a reference to his resurrection. As the risen Lord, he is the first to have been raised from the dead to ultimate glory (in glorified form). Calling Christ the "firstborn" Son is a reference to his resurrection from the dead as the divine Lord and not to a beginning in time.

As divine, Jesus redeemed us, but he did not do so alone. As we've implied here and there, he did so in loving interrelation with the heavenly Father and with the Holy Spirit. This topic of the Holy Spirit is the focus of our next chapter. Our insight into the very identity of God is not yet complete. We've only roared through one station after we boarded our train. There is another station yet ahead of us.

Study Questions:

1. Does the fact that God saves *through* Jesus mean that Jesus is not really the Savior? Explain your answer with examples from Scripture.

2. If Jesus is the Savior, must we say that he is also divine? Explain your answer.

3. How does Jesus save us? Explain your answer thoroughly.

4. How does Revelation 5 show us that Jesus must be divine?

5. How does John's Gospel show us that Jesus must be divine?

6. How do 2 Peter 1:1 and Titus 3:4 show us that Christ is divine?

7. What is the significance of saying that the Spirit of God is also the Spirit of Christ? Give other examples of how *God* and *Christ* are interchangeable terms in the New Testament.

8. What is the difference between prophets and the divine Son according to the New Testament?

5
STATION THREE
The Holy Spirit Saves

We boarded the train at the station named "Only God Saves." That took us by necessity to the station named "The Son Saves," affirming that Jesus is also to be regarded as divine. The same force of logic will take us to the next station, namely, "The Holy Spirit Saves," affirming that the Spirit is divine as well. This statement may sound strange to our ears, because, unlike the Scriptures about Jesus, the statement that the Spirit saves is not the typical language found in the Bible. But it is accurate in substance nevertheless.

Salvation Revisited

A young woman sat in my small office at the church that I pastored over thirty years ago. She was neatly dressed and proper and also very passionate about her faith. It was the heyday of what has been called the Charismatic movement in the mainline churches, and she had been swept up in the excitement of this new emphasis on the Holy Spirit in her mainline Protestant church. She was still loyal to her church and also active in a Charismatic prayer meeting that met weekly in her home. She was at my little church to invite me to her home study as a guest speaker.

In the process of inviting me, she couldn't resist explaining to me what the new emphasis on the life of the Holy Spirit had meant to her. She explained, "I was always accustomed to hearing sermons about the love of God or what Christ had done for me, but I still felt this emptiness inside. I also heard a lot about the importance of faith and the truthfulness of the Bible, but God still seemed so distant." What was revolutionary for her was the new stress that she had recently seen put on the Holy Spirit of God living within, making God near and present in a way that was strengthening and renewing. That she could be led of the Spirit and sensitive to this leading in relating to others made the life of faith a rich journey for her. Faith was no longer merely an intellectual assent to Christ or to the truths of the Bible but was now a yielding to the impulse of God's very presence embracing her and moving her to love others. I recall her saying, "The idea that I could cultivate a relationship with the Holy Spirit in my life was new to me. My devotion to Christ has taken on a newness and strength that I never experienced before."

The Holy Spirit is sometimes called the "shy" member of the Godhead, because the Spirit will testify of Christ (John 15:26). This point is vital because it shows that the Spirit does not save in isolation from the other persons of the Trinity but in loving interaction with them. The Spirit is poured forth from the heavenly Father to testify of the Son to the glory of the Father. The Holy Spirit draws creation into the loving embrace of the Father, Son, and Spirit. In doing this, the Spirit seeks to glorify the Father and the Son.

Yet this "shyness" of the Holy Spirit is not meant to imply that we are to ignore the Spirit. Salvation and the life of faith take on richer texture and substance once they are viewed through the lens of the work of the Holy Spirit. Indeed, the New Testament defines a Christian as someone who has become indwelled by the Holy Spirit through faith in Christ. Paul, for example, asked the Galatians, "Did you receive the Spirit by observing the law, or by believing what you heard? Are you so foolish? After beginning with the Spirit, are you now trying to attain your goal by human effort?" (Galatians 3:2). In other words, becoming a Christian in Paul's mind consists of receiving God's Holy Spirit within by faith in Christ rather than by human works. This divine presence in and among us represents the "down payment" of salvation, a salvation that will be fulfilled when the Spirit raises us from the dead with a body that is fully yielded to the Spirit and in the perfect image of Jesus (Ephesians 1:13–15; 2 Corinthians 5:1–5). This is salvation in the larger sense of the word and one way in which the Holy Spirit saves us.

Let's explore this point a bit further. We saw earlier that salvation is the victory of eternal life over sin and death. Humanity sinned against God and now exists in a condition of death: spiritual death (alienation from God) and physical death (the symptom of spiritual death). We saw that according to 2 Corinthians 5:1–5 we are bound by this condition of sin and death and we implicitly yearn for freedom—indeed, for the very life of the eternal Spirit. Let's look again at 2 Corinthians 5:1–5:

> Now we know that if the earthly tent we live in is destroyed, we have a building from God, an eternal house in heaven, not built by human hands. Meanwhile we groan, longing to be clothed with our heavenly dwelling, because when we are clothed, we will not be found naked.

For while we are in this tent, we groan and are burdened, because we do not wish to be unclothed but to be clothed with our heavenly dwelling, so that what is mortal may be swallowed up by life. Now it is God who has made us for this very purpose and has given us the Spirit as a deposit, guaranteeing what is to come.

The earthly tent in which we groan for freedom is the fleshly body bound by sin and death. The heavenly dwelling for which we groan is the spiritual body that we will have at the resurrection (Romans 8:22–23; 1 Corinthians 15:42–45). In the above-quoted text, Paul said that our earthly mortality will be "swallowed up by life" and said that this is the very purpose for which we were created. When we were created in Eden, we became living souls by the divine breath breathed within us (Genesis 2:7). After we fell into bondage to sin and death, this Spirit no longer indwelled us as a sanctifying force, though we continued to live and draw our breath from this divine presence (Acts 17:24–28). Bound to mortal existence subject to sin and death, we implicitly yearn for the indwelling of the Spirit to take us to the goal that God has intended for us from the beginning: not ideal natural existence, but even beyond to the spiritual body fully directed by the life of the Spirit and shaped to reflect the glory of the risen Jesus. *This* is salvation in the ultimate sense of the word according to the New Testament.

We can understand—in the light of how Spirit-oriented salvation is—why the gift of the Holy Spirit given to those who believe on Jesus is called the "deposit" or down payment of salvation. Notice Ephesians 1:13–14: "And you also were included in Christ when you heard the word of truth, the gospel of your salvation. Having believed, you were marked in him with a seal, the promised Holy Spirit, who is a deposit guaranteeing our inheritance until the redemption of those who are God's possession—to the praise of his glory."

Paul was using a financial metaphor in the above text. Just as in a business transaction a person may receive a down payment with a guarantee of payment to be given in full, so also God gives us the Holy Spirit within when we believe on Jesus. This gift of the Spirit is the seal of our covenant with Christ and the down payment of a guaranteed future salvation (the resurrection). In this future salvation we will experience the fullness of life in the Spirit—life in Christ's glorified image. In other words, the gift of the Holy Spirit within is the first stage of the future, full experience of the Spirit given to us in the spiritual body that we receive at the resurrection from the dead. For if the Spirit of God who raised Jesus from the dead dwells in us, this Spirit will raise us from the dead just as Christ himself was raised (Romans 8:11).

This powerful gift of new life in us leading to resurrection is powerfully foretold in the Old Testament in Ezekiel 37. The prophet Ezekiel was called of God to give hope to Israel during the nation's lowest point of disobedience and depression. There seemed to be no hope left for the nation. God gave Ezekiel a vision involving a valley of dry bones. The image is that of an army that had been caught and surrounded within a valley, a most hopeless situation. The Holy Spirit took Ezekiel back and forth throughout the valley to see the vast extent of the damage. Ezekiel noted, "I saw a great many bones on the floor of the valley, bones that were very dry" (Ezekiel 37:2). There was no life in them. Then God asked Ezekiel if these bones could live again. Stunned by the question, given the utter lifelessness of the bones, Ezekiel could only muster by way of response, "O Sovereign LORD, you alone know." (37:3).

Then God asked Ezekiel to prophesy to the bones. (Talk about preaching to a dead audience!) Ezekiel was to convey the following message from God: "Dry bones, hear the word of the LORD! . . . I will make breath enter you, and you will come to life" (37:4–5).

Then Ezekiel was to prophesy to the winds, which were a symbol of the breath or Spirit of God. This prophecy was more like a humble invocation, asking the Spirit to "breathe into these slain, that they may live" (37:9).

Then something amazing happened. The bones rose up as skeletons, took on flesh and blood, and became a mighty army for God (37:10). Then God not only promised to bring Israel as a restored nation back to their land, God said to them, "I am going to open your graves and bring you up from them" (37:12). God added, "Then you, my people, will know that I am the LORD, when I open your graves and bring you up from them" (37:13). The Spirit redeemed the people, restored them, and promised them the future resurrection from the dead.

When God raised Jesus from the dead by the Spirit (Romans 1:4), God showed that he was not just being figurative in Ezekiel 37. God was promising that the life of the Spirit in them would not only bring restoration and redemption in the here and now but also eternal life and victory over the grave. God meant this quite literally!

Now we are beginning to see how the Holy Spirit also saves. The Spirit is the one who perfects or completes the salvation willed by the Father and inaugurated by the Son's death and resurrection. The Spirit completes this salvation by bringing it to us and enabling us to participate in it. Without the Spirit, we would gaze on Jesus' death and resurrection from a distance, but we would have no direct relationship to it. We would remain bound in our condition of sin and death, still yearning for freedom but having no connection to it.

The Spirit brings the victory of Jesus' death and resurrection to our lives and allows us to experience it and be a part of it. Without the Holy Spirit, there would be no salvation. In fact, it was the Spirit that was the hidden potential of life at Jesus' crucifixion (Hebrews 9:14), because it was the Spirit that raised Jesus from the dead (Romans 1:4), in cooperation with the Father and with Jesus. It is then the Spirit that brings the victory of Jesus' death and resurrection to our lives when we believe in Jesus for salvation. Without the Spirit, there is no salvation. Not only Jesus saves, the Spirit saves, too.

So, the indwelling Holy Spirit is the down payment of future life in the here and now as well as the future reality of its payment in full (Ephesians 1:13–14). The Holy Spirit awakens us from spiritual death, a death that traps us within our self-centered existence. The Spirit allows us to put to death the self-centered self and awakens in us a self that is centered on Jesus and God's will for our lives. Our dominant question in life is no longer "What do I get out of it?" The major question by which we approach all situations is now "What does God will for me?"

This is what water baptism signifies, namely a dying to self (as we are buried with Christ in the water) and a rising again to a new life centered on Christ (coming up out of the water; see Romans 6:3–5). This new birth is what happens when the Spirit comes into us at the moment of our faith in Christ; we are born anew from above (John 1:12–13). The Holy Spirit binds us to Christ and indwells us at the moment of our initial faith in Christ and brings us into right relation with Christ (which is our justification). We are cleansed from all sin. The Spirit also sanctifies us by separating us from the bondage to sin and liberating us to live righteously for Christ. Paul could write, "But you were washed, you were sanctified, you were justified in the name of the Lord Jesus Christ and by the Spirit of our God" (1 Corinthians 6:11).

The Spirit continues by filling or renewing us afresh in our ability to bear witness to Christ as Savior and Lord before the world (Acts 1:8). When we grow weary or feel empty the Spirit renews us from within to become a powerful force for God again. The life of the Spirit is a continuous experience of overflowing love as we dedicate ourselves ever afresh to God and ever anew in service to others. Through the gift of the Spirit, the love of God is poured into us as a waterfall (Romans 5:5) and flows out from us like a gushing stream (John 7:37–38).

Once the Spirit enters us at the moment of our faith in Christ, the Spirit dwells or abides in us in representation of the presence of Christ (John 15:4). As the Spirit remains in us, he continues to give us fresh power, renewing us daily and flowing out from us. In other words, the Spirit lives in us as a dynamic fountain rather than as a static pond. Paul could speak of the Spirit's filling as an ongoing reality: "Be filled with the Spirit" (Ephesians 5:18). The command is present tense, meaning, "Be continuously filled with the Spirit!" How are we filled ever anew? We are filled by yielding to the Spirit in prayer and by responding positively to the Spirit's urges to love God and others.

The Spirit's flowing through us also changes us. We are transformed into the image of Jesus "with ever-increasing glory" (2 Corinthians 3:18). Christ is gradually formed in us (Galatians 4:19). This happens in our private prayer lives and in our study of God's Word, as God lifts the veil of misunderstanding and helps us to see the good news of Jesus in its pages (2 Corinthians 3:14–16). And it also happens as we see Jesus in one another in fellowship and submit to one another's ministry out of reverence for Christ (Ephesians 5:21).

The Holy Spirit works on our desires in order to uproot the self-centered and self-destructive passions of the flesh and to change them into passions that are consistent with the life and ministry of Jesus. This process occurs as we live by the Holy Spirit's leading. Paul wrote, "Live by the Spirit, and you will not gratify the desires of the sinful nature" (Galatians 5:16). Paul gave examples of desires and works of the sinful nature: "Sexual immorality, impurity and debauchery; idolatry and witchcraft; hatred, discord, jealousy, fits of rage, selfish ambition, dissensions, factions and envy; drunkenness, orgies, and the like" (Galatians 5:19–21). Examples of Christ-like desires and works of the Spirit are "love, joy, peace, patience, kindness, goodness, faithfulness, gentleness and self-control" (Galatians 5:22–23).

The Holy Spirit turns our deepest affections and yearnings into Christ-like desires. We are transformed from within. The new desires implanted by the Spirit and the works that they inspire are called spiritual "fruit" by Paul (Galatians 5:22). They are called fruit because they are nourished by God's Word and Spirit, and are cultivated by our obedient responses to the Spirit.

I recall once while I was a pastor during the 1970s that a man complained to me that the Holy Spirit was not changing him very much. But when I asked him how much he prayed or read God's Word, I received a blank stare (which told me everything I needed to know). When I asked him about his obedience to the voice of the Holy Spirit in loving and serving those in need, I received a vague response. It was clear to me that this person was not nearly as obedient to the leading of the Holy Spirit as he needed to be. None of us is perfect and we all fall short. Yet ongoing disobedience to the leading of the Spirit means that we are not yielding or submitting to what the Spirit wills to do in us. And we should not then be surprised that our growth in the life of the Holy Spirit is unusually sluggish.

Of course, growth in the life of the Holy Spirit is slow and gradual. This is why Paul likened it to fruit in Galatians 5. When people plant vineyards, they do not receive the harvest right away. Great patience is required, along with hard work. But the miracle of growth in a natural harvest is not something that comes primarily from us, but rather by the forces of nature. Spiritual growth also requires great patience and hard work on our part, but the growth comes from God as a miracle of his grace. The seed of the word of God is planted in us and watered by the life of the Holy Spirit. This is where growth really comes from. "I planted the seed, Apollos watered it," Paul wrote, "but God made it grow" (1 Corinthians 3:6).

Though we must be obedient to the Holy Spirit to grow, even this obedience is empowered by God. Nothing is earned by us or due fundamentally to our doing. It is all by God's grace, his undeserved favor. Paul wrote, "For it is by grace you have been saved, through faith—and this not from yourselves, it is the gift of God—not by works, so that no one can boast" (Ephesians 2:8–9). Indeed, everything comes from God's raising us up and giving us the power to respond favorably to grace: "Because of his great love for us, God, who is rich in mercy, made us alive with Christ even when we were dead in transgressions—it is by grace you have been saved" (Ephesians 2:4–5). In the end, everything is a gift of God. Let's talk more about the obedience to the Holy Spirit that God inspires in us.

Obedience to the Spirit

Obedience to the Holy Spirit begins with faith. Faith is trust in God, a deep trust of heart and mind that *submits to God's word and remains dependent on God for all things.* Faith is belief in Christ and a commitment to follow him as the Lord in all things. Faith is born the moment we accept Jesus as our Lord and Savior. It proceeds as hopeful trust in Christ, believing on God's promises granted to us in him. It can already grasp a foretaste of what the Lord has promised to give us in the resurrection of the dead. Faith reaches for that which is not yet visible. Faith is "being sure of what we hope for and certain of what we do not see" (Hebrews 11:1).

We receive the Holy Spirit by faith in Christ, and not by works. In fact, the Spirit inspires faith and enters us the moment we believe in Christ, for to belong to the Holy Spirit is also to belong to Christ (Romans 8:9). The gift of the Holy Spirit is never something that we can earn or deserve. As noted above, Paul asked the Christians who lived in the region of Galatia, "Did you receive the Spirit by observing the law, or by believing what you heard? Are you so foolish? After beginning with the Spirit, are you now trying to attain your goal by human effort?" (Galatians 3:2–3).

The Galatian Christians were thinking that they could earn God's blessings by obeying the law. Paul made it clear that this was impossible, for there is no commandment that can give new life (Galatians 3:21). The law points to new life in God by urging us to love God with our entire being and promising a blessing to those who do (Deuteronomy 6:4–5; 30:16). In reality, the law helps to guide and to cultivate this life once it is received, but obedience to the law cannot grant such life. Only the Spirit of God can do this (Ezekiel 36:27). Paul found it absurd that some believed they could earn the Holy Spirit by works of the law. The Holy Spirit is not ours to earn or to master. It is the gift of God's own presence received by faith in Christ.

Paul then asked, "Are you so foolish?" Since the Holy Spirit was originally received by faith in Christ and not by obedience to the law, we should not think that the life of the Spirit is perfected by anything but faith either. In other words, faith is the means by which the life of the Spirit is received and by which it grows in us. The entire span of the life in the Spirit is sustained by an ongoing and growing faith in Christ. It is never earned or deserved. It is received and continuously embraced by loyal and undying trust in Christ and in the fulfillment of God's promises in him.

Faith also involves repentance. Repentance is "godly sorrow" for sin. Godly sorrow depends on the conviction of the Holy Spirit in response to the word of God. It is not destructive, but constructive and healing. It cuts our hearts like a surgeon's scalpel with the goal of new life and healing. As Paul wrote, "Godly sorrow brings repentance that leads to salvation and leaves no regret, but worldly sorrow brings death" (2 Corinthians 7:10). Yet repentance is not only sorrow for sin but also a turning away from sin in disgust and a turning to Christ in trusting faith. Paul proclaimed in Acts, "I have declared to both Jews and Greeks that they must turn to God in repentance and have faith in our Lord Jesus" (Acts 20:21). The obedience involved in the life of the Holy Spirit is the obedience of faith *and* repentance. This turning to God in faith and repentance is the nature of conversion. Conversion is a one-time event, and it is also an ongoing reality. We are always turning away from sin and turning to God in trust and obedience.

It is important to see faith and repentance as inseparable and integral aspects of one larger act of turning to God. If we do not do this, it will be possible to see repentance as the separate and necessary requirement *before* we can have faith. Repentance then becomes a requirement that we have to adequately fulfill before we are worthy of faith, making works the requirement for faith. But such would be contrary to the nature of faith. Faith is not a prize that can be won once a person has cried, wailed, and done sufficiently penitential acts. Though an act of obedience, faith is foundationally a gift given to us by the word of God: "Faith comes from hearing the message, and the message is heard through the word of Christ" (Romans 10:17). The convicting power of the Holy Spirit allows the word of God to come alive in us as a source of grace in converting to God, for the Scriptures are "God-breathed" (2 Timothy 3:15–16). No amount of wailing or other deeds can make us worthy of this faith. If we see repentance as an inseparable part of faith itself, we can then recognize that both—acting together—are responses to the word of God and the power of the Holy Spirit. Both are empowered by the word of God and the Holy Spirit, and both are gifts of God.

Faith and repentance are the foundation of all obedience to the Spirit's leading. All submission to the Spirit's work in us through good works flows from faith and repentance. Faith takes no credit for itself but depends wholly on God for all things. Faith is not a work (though it requires obedience); it is sort of like an "anti-work," because it trusts wholly in the work of another. Faith is not exercised from our own power. It is a Spirit-motivated turning to God with empty hands in order to receive all things from God's hands. We simply yield and accept the gifts of God. Faith naturally leads to good works but is not itself a work. It's more like open arms to receive God's loving embrace. The saving work of the Spirit does not end with justification and sanctification by faith, though it begins and progresses from there. It goes even beyond that to the resurrection of the body. The resurrection is the ultimate of life in the Spirit, the ultimate in glorified existence in Christ's image.

Glorification

As noted earlier in this chapter, the final perfection of the Spirit's saving work is through glorification. Paul wrote concerning God's saving work in us that "those he called, he also justified; those he justified, he also glorified" (Romans 8:30). Glorification is being raised from the dead by the Spirit of God in the perfect image of the risen Christ. The Spirit's presence in us is the down payment and the guarantee of this future glory (Ephesians 1:13–14). Right now we fall short of this glory because of sin (Romans 3:23). But one day we will be freed from sin and death and will be able to gain the liberty of a body wholly given over to the life of the Spirit, a spiritual body yielded to the Spirit in a way that is not possible for us now. At that time, mortality will be entirely taken up into the immortal life of God (2 Corinthians 5:5).

The resurrection of the dead is connected in the Bible with Jesus' return at the end of time. In 1 Thessalonians 4:16 Paul wrote, "For the Lord himself will come down from heaven, with a loud command, with the voice of the archangel and with the trumpet call of God, and the dead in Christ will rise first." John 5:25 states something similar: "I tell you the truth, a time is coming and has now come when the dead will hear the voice of the Son of God and those who hear will live." The question that is often posed is what exactly happens to Christians at death, prior to Christ's return. Some believe that we simply go out of existence at death but that God will recreate us at resurrection (God has the precise genetic information necessary to do this). Others believe that the souls of the righteous dead "sleep" in a deep slumber until Christ returns, and are awakened at resurrection. Paul did refer to those who are "asleep" in Christ (1 Thessalonians 4:13), though this reference seems to be just a figurative term for death. In my view, the Bible indicates that the soul goes to heaven at death in some sort of disembodied state (as a spiritual essence) to enjoy heaven and to await resurrection into a spiritual body at the end of time. Paul implied as much in Philippians 1:23 when he defined death as a "departure" to be "with Christ." So it seems to be the case that the disembodied souls return with Christ from heaven at his coming only to rise from the earth in glorified (spiritual) bodies.

The point here is that salvation is not fulfilled until the resurrection of the dead. In fact, Paul indicated that our adoption as God's children is not official until then. Paul wrote, "We ourselves, who have the firstfruits of the Spirit, groan inwardly as we wait eagerly for our adoption as sons, the redemption of our bodies" (Romans 8:23). Notice that we are still waiting for our adoption as God's children and that this adoption is identified as the "redemption of our bodies," which most certainly refers to the resurrection. Yet just eight verses back, Paul said that we *already* are the children of God because the Spirit of God's Son, Jesus Christ, dwells in us (8:15–16). This is the dynamic tension between the "now" and the "not yet" of salvation in the Holy Spirit. Salvation is "now" because we possess the Spirit of life already within, and salvation is also "not yet" because the Spirit has not yet raised us from the dead in the perfect image of the glorified Christ, in perfect submission to the life of the Spirit.

The Spirit will not only raise the dead one day, the Spirit will also create a new heavens and new earth. Salvation is not an escape of the soul from creation. Redemption includes the remaking of this world, of our bodies as well as the entire cosmos, into the glorious image of Jesus. This is the victory of God's immortal life over sin and death, the perfect yielding of creation to the Spirit of God. So it seems perfectly clear that the Spirit is just as much an agent of salvation as the Father and the Son.

The Spirit Is Divine

If *only* God saves, if *only* God gives new life, and the Holy Spirit saves and gives new life, then the Spirit must be divine. There is no possibility of any exception to this rule. If the Spirit were not divine, then the possibility would exist that there would be a source of salvation besides God. This is an utter impossibility. Only the Creator can make all things new; only God can grant new life. If the Spirit gives new life, the Spirit must be divine. Our train that has departed from the station "Only God Can Save" has taken us inescapably to the station named "The Holy Spirit Saves." And because the Scriptures support the claim that the Spirit saves, the Holy Spirit is God.

It is important at this point to also defend the personhood of the Spirit. We made a few remarks in this area earlier, but something more elaborate is needed here. The reason is that the personhood of the Father and the Son is not generally in dispute. The fact that they have a personal relationship and act as persons is usually not denied. But the Holy Spirit has tended in some quarters to be regarded as the impersonal presence or power of God. Likened in Scripture to the breath or power of God, it seems to some that the Holy Spirit is not a person.

Yet the Holy Spirit can be grieved (Isaiah 63:10; Ephesians 4:30), lied to (Acts 5:3), and blasphemed (Matthew 12:31), which only makes sense if the Spirit is a person. The Spirit also speaks (Acts 1:16; 28:25; 1 Timothy 4:1; Revelation 2:7), speaking only "what he hears" (John 16:13); testifies (Romans 8:16; Hebrews 10:15; 1 John 5:6); wills or determines (1 Corinthians 12:11); contends (Genesis 6:3); reveals (Luke 2:26; 1 Corinthians 2:10; Ephesians 3:5); intercedes (Romans 8:27); convicts (John 16:8); and even searches out the deep things of God for us (1 Corinthians 2:10). These activities are certainly those done by a *personal* agent. The fact that the Spirit intercedes for us to God the Father or searches out the deep things of God the Father implies that the Spirit is a personal agent *distinct* from the heavenly Father.

The fact that the Spirit will not speak "on his own" but will only communicate what belongs to Christ (John 16:13–14) is strong proof that the Spirit is also distinct as a personal agent from the Son of God. The Spirit testifies of Christ, not speaking "on his own" but seeking only to bring him glory (John 15:26; 16:14), which would make no sense if the Spirit were indistinguishable from the Son. If they were indistinguishable, why is a word spoken against Jesus forgiven but not a word spoken against the Holy Spirit (Matthew 12:32)? The phrase "the Lord, who is the Spirit" (2 Corinthians 3:18) is arguably a reference to the lordship actually exercised by the Holy Spirit in harmony with that which is exercised by the Son.

That the Spirit is divine is taught in Scripture where Peter notes that lying to the Holy Spirit is lying to God (Acts 5:3–4). Besides, the Spirit does what only God can do: creates, creates anew, sanctifies, glorifies, raises people from the dead, reveals the deep things of God, and so on. If the Spirit does what only God can do as an agent of salvation, the Spirit is by nature divine. There is simply no other possibility.

Can We Pray to the Holy Spirit?

I sometimes get a question about why we don't generally pray to the Holy Spirit. There is no case in the Bible in which the Holy Spirit is addressed in prayer. Usually, prayers are directed to the Father in Jesus' name or to Jesus, to the ultimate glory of the Father. But the Holy Spirit is not addressed in prayer. Why is that? Surely as divine the Holy Spirit can be the object of prayer.

The reason that the Holy Spirit is not addressed in prayer in the Scripture is that the Spirit functions as the person of the Godhead who empowers prayer from within us. The Holy Spirit and the bride of Christ together invoke Christ to come (Revelation 22:17). It is only by the Spirit that we can confess Christ as Lord to the glory of the Father (1 Corinthians 12:3; Philippians 2:11). The Spirit helps us in our weakness by interceding to God through our groaning and sighing for the redemption yet to come (Romans 8:26–27). We always "pray in the Spirit on all occasions with all kinds of prayers and requests" (Ephesians 6:18). Since the Holy Spirit is the one who draws us to Christ and through him to the heavenly Father, the Spirit is not generally the *object* of prayer. This has to do with the Spirit's function and not with the Spirit's nature (which is divine and worthy of prayer). The Spirit is the power of God's presence from which we pray. The Holy Spirit's role in prayer reminds us that prayer is completely in God: to, through, and by God. There is no way that we can take any steps towards God in our own power.

Yet, though it is not generally natural to pray to the Holy Spirit, given the Spirit's role as the divine power from which we pray, there is nothing in Scripture *against* this practice or that would in principle discourage us from doing this. The invocation of the Holy Spirit (inviting the Holy Spirit to be among us in worship or at the Lord's Supper) has been a standard practice historically in many churches. In a sense, the bride of Christ says, "Come," to the Spirit before joining with the Spirit to say, "Come," to Christ. Since the Holy Spirit speaks to the church on behalf of Christ (Revelation 3:6), why not invite the Spirit along with inviting Christ? If Christ was knocking on the door of the church of Laodicea through the voice of the Spirit (Revelation 3:20), wouldn't it be allowed to invoke the Spirit in inviting Christ among us? After all, there is nothing in principle wrong with this, especially since the Holy Spirit is the one who represents Christ's presence among us. So the Spirit as well as Christ exercises lordship, in harmony with Christ (2 Corinthians 3:18).

There would also be nothing in principle wrong with glorifying the Holy Spirit, along with Jesus and the heavenly Father, as Lord and God. The Holy Spirit is divine and represents Christ among us. In glorifying Christ or the heavenly Father through Christ, we implicitly glorify the Holy Spirit anyway. We might as well make that explicit on occasion and mention this in prayer and in worship. It may not be the natural thing to do, given the tendency to simply pray by the power or agency of the Holy Spirit. But doing something that might seem a bit awkward does not make it wrong.

Indeed, the Spirit may be the "shy" member of the Godhead, the one who graciously functions as our experiential point of contact with Christ and the heavenly Father through Christ. The Spirit represents Christ's presence among us as the one from whom we address Christ and the one by whom Christ addresses us. But the so-called "shyness" of the Spirit is no reason for us to completely neglect acknowledging the Spirit's role as the "go-between" God. We don't want to deceive ourselves into thinking that we can embrace Christ or hear his words in our own strength.

Without this go-between God, Christ would be a figure in a history book rather than a living voice who encounters us with words of challenge and comfort, drawing us into a life of obedience and blessing. If Christ grants clear (objective) definition and direction to the Holy Spirit's work, the Spirit works to make Christ a living presence in which we participate by faith. Invoking or glorifying the Holy Spirit on occasion can remind us of the importance of the Holy Spirit among us as the very presence of God and as our entry into God's loving embrace. In interactive communion with the Father and the Son, the Spirit saves and is therefore divine.

Study Questions:

1. Use 2 Corinthians 5:1–5, Ephesians 1:13–14, and Ezekiel 37 in order to show how Spirit-oriented salvation is.

2. Explain the Spirit's work in new birth, justification, sanctification, renewal (filling), and glorification.

3. Explain how the Spirit causes us to become more like Christ (forming Christ in us).

4. Explain the teaching of Galatians 5 about spiritual fruit.

5. Discuss the meaning of faith and repentance as foundational acts of obedience to the Spirit.

6. Give scriptural evidence for the fact that the Spirit is a personal agent distinct from the persons of the Father and the Son.

7. Why is it an inescapable conclusion that the Spirit is divine?

6
END STATION
God Is a Trinity

We've now reached our end station. Step off the train and the sign above will read, "God Is a Trinity." We've arrived here of necessity, by force of logic, the logic of faith. There has been no way to exit the train or to steer it onto a different track, not if we wanted to remain in the direction determined by our premise and the station where we originally boarded the train. Again, given the fact that both the Scriptures and the church assume that salvation is provided by God alone as the Father, the Son, and the Holy Spirit, it is clear that all three must equally be this God; all three together must be a trinity. Why is this the case? The reason is the basic premise repeated throughout our discussion leading up to this chapter—namely, *only God can save.* There are no exceptions to this rule, for any assumption of a Savior besides God is idolatrous—plain and simple. Since only the one God can save, and the Father, the Son, and the Holy Spirit save in loving interaction, the one God must be a loving interaction of Father, Son, and Spirit. This is how we've arrived at this end station called "God Is a Trinity."

Some, however, would still question our logic. Does the belief that Father, Son, and Holy Spirit are God lead *necessarily* to belief in the Trinity? Some would say, for example, that our logic could easily lead to a belief in three separate gods, which would not be Trinitarian (belief in one God who is three) but tritheistic (belief in three separate gods). Is this so?

Three Gods?

It was my first semester at Wheaton College. The year was 1974. I had just graduated from college and was eager to do a master's degree is systematic theology. I had no idea at that time that this course of study would lead me to another master's degree at Union Theological Seminary (at Columbia University) and to a doctorate in theology at the historic University of Basel (Switzerland). I was wet behind the ears but willing to grow. I sat in the first session of a memorable course in historical theology under Robert Webber. He turned out to be one of my all-time favorite professors. I mention him here because of what he said that day. It was something that I never forgot (one of a number of things he said that I never forgot). He said that in practice many Christians are *tritheists*. We tend to think of God as a pantheon of three separate gods: Father, Son, and Holy Spirit. The oneness of God tends to elude us. We just don't think about it.

I was stunned by this remark, and I couldn't help but think that he was right. Growing up in the church, I tended to think of God the Father as the chief God, sort of like Zeus sitting high on his throne and ruling all things. Then the Holy Spirit and the Son of God were sort of like his underlings or his ambassadors or assistants, who went about fulfilling what the Father willed for them to do. It was only later that I realized how thoroughly monotheistic the Old Testament faith was and how deeply entrenched Trinitarian theology was in this monotheistic confession. Indeed, Karl Barth was right; the Trinitarian theology of the early church was not bent primarily on supporting God's plurality, but rather on defending God's unity (God is one) in the light of the divine plurality clearly revealed in the story of Jesus. Trinitarian theology did not primarily want to say, "Here is how God is plural," but rather, "In the light of the relationships of Father, Son, and Holy Spirit, here is how God is one." Take away monotheism (belief in one God), and there is no Trinitarianism.

In this light, we need to look at the challenge of some who might note at this point in our discussion that the deity of the Father, the Son, and the Holy Spirit does not yet constitute a trinity. For example, if there were three separate gods, there would not be Trinitarianism (one God in three persons), but rather tritheism (three gods). Could it then be that the Father, the Son, and the Holy Spirit are three separate individuals, three separate gods? If so, our end station would not be "God Is a Trinity"; it would read "Three Gods" or "Tritheism." What is it about our station of departure (our premise) that rules out tritheism as a legitimate end station?

We addressed this issue briefly in our first chapter. Let us take this issue up again here but with greater detail. Keep in mind that our premise, our station of departure, is biblical and uncompromising: God alone is the Lord of life and salvation. There is no possibility for competition by other gods. Implied in this premise, therefore, is a monotheistic faith, or a faith in only one God. Our biblical premise, the station from which we started our trip, does not say that only the gods (plural) can save, that if one of the three persons does not appeal to us, we can go to one of the other two for salvation. No! The first station of our journey states clearly that only God (singular) alone can save and that there is *no other Savior*, no other Lord of life and salvation. It is either this God of creation (and of the exodus), or it is alienation and death. There are no other possibilities. The logic of faith won't allow it. The station of "Only God Can Save" and the stations claiming that Father, Son, and Holy Spirit all save cannot lead to the conclusion that there are many gods. That would be to deviate from the track that proceeds from our first station.

The premise that only God can save is expressed in the Old Testament with monotheistic language. Notice how God the only Savior speaks in the first person singular ("I") in Scripture to say that "I am the LORD, and there is no other; apart from me there is no God" (Isaiah 45:5). If there were three separate gods, there would be no convincing way to explain the first person singular pronoun in the context of this verse. The grammar of the verse would be misleading. The verse would say instead, "We are the LORDs." So, if there is a plurality of gods claiming the privilege to save, how many more might be admitted to this pantheon worthy of devotion and praise? We can see where this might take us.

The biblical insistence that the God of the exodus alone can save (Hosea 13:4) and that besides this God there are no others (Isaiah 45:5) would become meaningless verbiage. Indeed, Deuteronomy 6:4 expresses the basic creed of the Israelite people: "Hear, O Israel: The LORD our God, the LORD is one." The LORD (singular) is *one*. The reason for this affirmation is given in the following verse (6:5): "Love the LORD your God with all your heart and with all your soul and with all your strength." In other words, there is no possibility of divided loyalty (choosing between two or more different gods), because there is only *one* Lord of all. We must devote all loyalty only to this one God, or we are lost.

The first person singular pronoun does not indicate three separate gods, even if they were unified in will or purpose. Clearly, the God of Scripture always speaks in the first person singular when addressing humanity. This is one of the cardinal principles of Trinitarian theology drawn from Scripture. Any use of the plural in divine speech (e.g., "Let us make man in our image," Genesis 1:26) represents a conversation *internal* to God and not between God and another. The first person singular when addressing someone *external* to God shows that God is truly one, while the plural pronoun of conversation *internal* to God shows a complexity to this oneness that allows there to be three.

The universal use of the first person singular in divine speech directed outside of God strongly indicates that God is a *single being*. There is no way, in my view, of remaining completely loyal to the language of Scripture unless we insist on this as a basic component of our view of God and of the premise in our journey. The idea of a pantheon of gods or polytheism (belief in more than one god) is pagan, foreign to the heart of Old Testament faith and the history of Israelite religion. Indeed, God said, "There is no God apart from me, a righteous God and a Savior; there is none but me." (Isaiah 45:21).

Demigods?

Some may not yet be satisfied that the end station of "God Is a Trinity" is really the logical outcome of the story of Jesus. Given the fact that God is one, could we not say that only the heavenly Father is truly divine and that Jesus is only a demigod, a semi-divine being, or an exalted creature who has god-like qualities but who is not really divine? Then we could make the Holy Spirit an impersonal power exuded from God's presence or maybe a demigod as well. In this way, we could preserve the teaching that God is only one. This heresy, called *subordinationism* (because it radically subordinates the Son and the Spirit to God), was represented by Arius and some others in the fourth century and is still present among some today.

This alternative, as we have seen, is not biblical. I recall one bright Saturday morning playing monopoly with my two daughters (then six and eight) when I was suddenly interrupted by a knock at the door. As I opened the door I was met by a polite greeting from two neatly dressed men, a younger man who seemed to lead the team and an older man who appeared to be the less experienced of the two. They introduced themselves as students of the Bible and asked me if I would be interested in studying the Bible with them. It did not take me long to realize that they were Jehovah's Witnesses.

Jehovah's Witnesses are indeed sincere but their view of Christ is not adequate as a biblical portrayal of who he is. They regard him to be an exalted creature (an angel) but not as truly divine in nature. I recall sharing this criticism with them. To save time, I directed their attention to Hosea 13:4 and to the biblical teaching that only *God* can save. I then directed them to 2 Timothy 1:10 and to several other texts that clearly portray Jesus as the Savior or that admonish us to trust in him or worship him as Savior. The younger man was bright and grasped my point immediately. If only God is to be trusted and worshiped as Savior, and Jesus is trusted and worshiped as Savior, Jesus must be truly divine. The only way that I can describe the look on his face as he grasped this point was that of a fox caught in a trap. He immediately tried every which way to be free of this biblical logic.

"Well," he said, "we consider Jesus as being very close to God, the most exalted of all beings." I immediately responded that worshiping or trusting in *any* being besides God for salvation is not allowed in Scripture, no matter how exalted. He then said, "But God saves *through* Jesus!" I then directed his attention to texts which state that Jesus saves, too. He responded very quickly (as though trying numerous approaches to the problem as they came to his mind), "But Jesus helps us in salvation and can be viewed as a Savior *in a sense*, but the ultimate Savior is God alone." There was no way to wiggle out in this way, since the Scriptures are quite specific about how Jesus saves and note that Jesus saves in precisely the same way that God saves, namely by canceling sin and conquering death (e.g., 2 Timothy 1:10).

That's hardly an auxiliary function! For this reason, Jesus is worshiped in Scripture with the exact same praise that is given to the heavenly Father: "To him who sits on the throne and to the Lamb be praise and honor and glory" (Revelation 5:13).

The younger man saw that our argument was not proceeding well for him, so he gave me some literature and left. Soon afterwards, my older daughter pointed out to me that the two men were out in the street engaged in a vigorous discussion. It seemed that the older man was himself provoked to question the Jehovah's Witness teaching and the younger one was now vigorously attempting to keep him in the fold. Before I had the chance to open the door, they had proceeded down the street. It seems that I had caused some unrest in their day.

It was my purpose to create some unrest, for God often uses such unrest to speak to us all. There is simply no way of qualifying Jesus as a demigod and still expect him to function as the Savior and ultimate hope of the people of God. For the creation is infinitely "other" than God and not qualified to save or worthy of praise (Romans 1:21–23). Even the most exalted creature with the brightest god-like qualities falls infinitely short of functioning as the Savior of humankind or as the recipient of our trust for salvation and of our worship. There is simply no way of having the cake and eating it, too. If Jesus is not truly divine, he cannot be the Savior, as the Scriptures say he is.

The same reasoning applies to the Holy Spirit. As we noted, the Spirit is a person, for he wills (1 Corinthians 12:11), searches (1 Corinthians 2:10), intercedes (Romans 8:26), testifies (Romans 8:16), and can be lied to (Acts 5:3) and grieved (Ephesians 4:30). This Spirit saves in the sense of perfecting salvation in sanctifying and glorifying flesh by indwelling creation and raising people from the dead. So the Spirit is fully divine as well.

Are there any other alternatives to the belief in the Trinity?

Three Manifestations of One God?

Given that neither tritheism nor subordinationism is the logical outcome of our stations, is there another non-Trinitarian alternative? Someone might hesitate here and point out that perhaps the Trinity is not the logical end station after all, because the work of the Father, the Son, and the Holy Spirit does not involve *three distinct persons* as Trinitarian theology maintains. If only God can save and this God is one God, then how can there be three divine persons at work in salvation? By ending at the "God Is a Trinity" station, have we deviated from the direction determined by our original station, our original premise? Is another alternative possible?

This question brings us now to the most difficult part of our discussion and we must proceed carefully, in a way that is faithful to the teaching of Scripture and to the logic of the biblical premise that we have been working with throughout our discussion. Keep in mind that the Scriptures clearly present Father, Son, and Holy Spirit as active in salvation. Since only God saves, and Father, Son, and Holy Spirit save, the one God must also be seen as three. The conclusion that we will need to reach is that the one God, who alone saves at the exclusion of any others, saves as an *interaction* of *three*: Father, Son, and Holy Spirit.

But how does this one God involve three? Some have sought from a desire for consistency to deny that Father, Son, and Holy Spirit are eternally distinct persons. The terms *Father*, *Son*, and *Holy Spirit* are rather three functions or manifestations of the one God. For example, I am a father, a son, and a friend. These are different roles that I play as a single person. Similarly, Father, Son, and Holy Spirit are three temporal functions of the one God in action within various circumstances.

We need to point out from the start that the above view (called *modalism*) can still represent a Trinitarian theology of sorts, since it can note (if so interpreted) that God acts in our history as Father, Son, and Holy Spirit. By denying that these three functions have an eternal basis within God, modalism is out of step with the full doctrine of the Trinity as taught in Scripture and as affirmed in the mainstream of Trinitarian theology historically. But even the modalist can be prone to conclude that, at the very least, the one God functions in the story of Jesus as Father, Son, and Holy Spirit. Yet is this enough to describe our end station? Are all of the implications of our stations preserved in this modalistic view of God?

Modalism may account for our first station, our premise that only the one God revealed in the exodus can save. The problem for modalism arises with the following three stations that appear down the track, the ones that note that the Father saves, the Son saves, and the Spirit saves, meaning that all three are divine. As we noted each step of the way, the Father, Son, and Spirit save in loving interaction with each other. The story of Jesus that provides the context (or narrative "geography") for these three stations indicates that Father, Son, and Holy Spirit save not in isolation from each other but precisely within a loving interaction with each other.

The problem with modalism in its possible place as our end station is the fact that manifestations or functions cannot relate to each other, cannot love one another. My roles as a father, a son, and a friend cannot love each other. Only different persons can do that. *Yet the Bible is clear that Father, Son, and Holy Spirit do interact lovingly with each other.* The biblical use of the first person singular for God when God addresses those external to God's self is not the whole story. God also interacts within God's self as three, even using the plural pronoun within internal conversation: "Let us make man in our image" (Genesis 1:26), and, "The LORD said, 'Let us go down and confuse their language'" (Genesis 11:6–7). Indeed, the Father loved the Son from before the time in which the worlds were made (John 17:24).

Some who see Father, Son, and Holy Spirit as mere manifestations tend to restrict Jesus' love for the Father to Jesus' humanity in order to account for the interpersonal nature of that love without assuming that there can be an interpersonal relationship within God. But this maneuver assumes wrongly that Jesus could momentarily lay his divine self aside and act independently of it. Such is impossible, since it is the very divine Word or Son of the Father who took on flesh as a tent or dwelling place (John 1:14). This fleshly tent cannot now act independently of the Son incarnate within it! If the Son loves the Father, it is the divine Son loving the divine Father, two divine persons in loving interaction.

Indeed, if we allow Jesus to love the Father as the divine Son of God, then we cannot avoid a love relationship between two divine agents. And if the Spirit is seen as the essence of this love and as one who participates in it, three interactive persons end up being involved in God. A modalist might say at this point that perhaps the one person of God loves God's self in the functions of Father, Son, and Holy Spirit. My response would be that if we view these functions of Father, Son, and Holy Spirit as eternally distinct (as Scripture indicates in John 17:24) we are definitely within the realm of Trinitarian theology (even if the term *persons* is not used of the three).

But let's pause here for a moment to see if a single self-interactive person is an adequate model for understanding the robust and free interaction between the Father and the Son by means of the Holy Spirit, such as we have depicted in the story of Jesus (Matthew 3:16–17). Does this single-person model adequately account for the interactive love shared freely among the three divine agents of Father, Son, and Holy Spirit? If I love myself, I do not do so as two or three distinct agents but rather as one agent reflecting on myself. As such, the agent loving me does not act freely in any way distinct from me but rather in a way wholly determined by me as a self-determined person (singular).

Yet Jesus as the divine Son of the Father does act freely vis-à-vis the heavenly Father, freely choosing out of obedience to do the will of the Father on earth, even experiencing agony over this decision (as in the garden of Gethsemane, Mark 14:35–36, or the cry to the Father from the cross over the experience of forsakenness from the Father, Mark 15:33–34). Although it is unimaginable that the Son could act contrary to the Father, he still acted freely in a way that seems too distinct from the Father to be described adequately within a one-person model. In fact, Hebrews 2:5–7 indicates that this free obedience by the Son towards the Father characterized the Son's coming into the world to inhabit a fleshly body, even predating the obedience that would characterize the life of Jesus as the incarnation of the divine Son. Note this text:

> Therefore, when Christ came into the world, he said:
>   "Sacrifice and offering you did not desire,
>   but a body you prepared for me;
>   with burnt offerings and sin offerings
>   you were not pleased.
>   Then I said, 'Here I am—it is written about me in
>   the scroll—
>   I have come to do your will, O God.'"
> (Hebrews 10:5–7)

Though this text involves the God-man Jesus' obedience to the Father, the decision to obey is also described as involving the divine Son's incarnation into flesh, as something motivating the Son's *coming into the world* to inhabit the body prepared for him (by the Holy Spirit, Luke 1:35).

Of course, we will rightly note that God's personhood is infinitely more complex than ours. Could it not be that the *one* being of God can love God's self in a way that is so complex that it involves three eternally distinct agents who act freely towards one another? Of course! This is exactly the case, which is why we need to be careful not to confine God to the inadequate model of one human person's loving himself (or herself). This is also why it would help us to refer to the Father, the Son, and the Holy Spirit as persons of the *one being* of God in order to preserve the true complexity and richness of the interaction of the three. But we must be careful not to see these persons as separate individuals but merely as acting personal agents. The persons of Father, Son, and Holy Spirit are *distinct* but also *inseparable*.

Therefore, the premise that only God can save demands at first the God (singular) of Israel in the Old Testament as the one and only Savior. But once we realize from Scripture that the Father saves, the Son saves, and the Holy Spirit saves, and that all three save *as interacting persons*, the end station necessarily signifies the one God as consisting of three eternally *distinct* persons, namely the Trinity. The premise that only God can save ends up being described in the Bible with Trinitarian specificity that preserves both singularity of being and a fascinating interaction among three, Father, Son, and Holy Spirit. This is the nature of the track that takes us to "God Is a Trinity" station. Given the assumptions of Scripture, the track from our original station could not have led in any other direction.

Does the language of Scripture lead to the conclusion that the one being of God exists as three eternally distinct (though inseparable) persons who save in loving interaction with each other? From time eternal, the divine Word (or Son) of God was "with" God the Father (John 1:1, see also v. 18). The Son was the agent through whom the heavenly Father created all things (John 1:3; Colossians 1:16; Hebrews 1:2); the Holy Spirit was there too according to Genesis 1:2. Before the worlds were made, the Son shared the eternal glory of deity with the Father (John 17:5), which is the divine love that characterizes the essence of the Holy Spirit (John 17:24; Romans 5:5). As the Father sent the Son into the world out of love for humankind (John 3:16), the Son devoted himself to the will of the Father in the earthly body prepared for him (Hebrews 10:5–7). The Holy Spirit facilitated the conception of the Son in Mary's womb (Luke 1:35).

It is clear that before all things, the Father, the Son, and the Holy Spirit existed as an interactive circle of love. We gain an insight into this interactive circle of love at Jesus' baptism. There Jesus is baptized out of devotion to the will of the Father just as the Father poured out the Holy Spirit on him while saying, "This is my Son whom I love; with him I am well pleased" (Matthew 3:16–17). Just as was the case before the worlds were made, Jesus as the incarnation of the divine Son shared at his baptism the glory and love of the Holy Spirit with the heavenly Father. This interaction among the three persons characterized Jesus' entire life according to the Gospels.

This intimacy between the persons, however, is pierced by the sword of suffering and alienation at the cross of Christ. Even as Jesus descended into the darkness of human sin and death and cried out the question as to why the Father had abandoned him (Mark 15:34), the Spirit was there as the hidden promise of eternal life (Hebrews 9:14). The event of the cross is covered in darkness. It seemed that all was lost. But the resurrection revealed that the cross was actually a hidden victory in the making (so to speak). The presence of the eternal Spirit at the cross (as Hebrews 9:14 indicates) shows us that the power of eternal life was already at work (only hidden) at the time of the cross.

Because of this, we can also say that the power of new life is hidden within our dark moments, too. The power of new life will manifest itself in time if we wait on God. Jesus recognized this shortly after his death, as his soul expressed confidence from the realm of the dead that the Father would not abandon him to the grave (Acts 2:27). In three days, the Father raised Jesus from the dead by the agency of the Spirit as proof that the Father had not abandoned Jesus to the grave (Romans 1:4). That same promise that God will not abandon us, either, is given to all who by faith in Jesus possess the Spirit of God (Romans 8:11). After Jesus rose and ascended to the right hand of the Father, he received the Holy Spirit from the Father once more to fully share again in the glory of Father. He then poured forth this Spirit on us so that we could share in his victory over sin and death (Acts 2:33).

The story of Jesus makes it abundantly clear that the one God who saves is an interactive circle of love consisting of Father, Son, and Holy Spirit. This is the nature of our end station. There was no way—given the first station and the stations through which our train has proceeded—that the end station could have been any different. The logic of faith has followed its necessary course.

One in Three?

This concept of the one God in three distinct persons seems to be a difficult pill for many to swallow. It seems like a mathematical absurdity to say that one can be three and three can be one. This is why we are sometimes accused of being tritheists after all. Though this charge is unfounded as a description of Trinitarian theology, it may be accurate as a response to how many Christians have described the Trinity on a popular level. For example, I've heard Christians refer to three separate or individual "people" in one God. "Three separate and individual people" is tritheistic and is not, properly speaking, Trinitarian. Here is where Christians have to be very precise about their language so as not to mislead people. Trinitarian theology refers to the one God as existing eternally in three distinct (not "separate" and not separable) persons.

Our caution concerning how we are to understand our end station does not add much clarity to how God can be three *and* one. In fact, we are confronted even more intensely with our mathematical problem. I recall a worried mother e-mailing me once about her college-aged son. He had taken a course from a professor at a secular college that led him to believe that the theologians of the early church must have been drunk when they arrived at such a ridiculous understanding of God as a trinity. How could one being exist as three eternally distinct and interacting persons? This idea seemed to this young man to be confused, as though the people who had come up with it could not decide if God was meant to be one or three, so they made God both!

I tried to help the woman respond to the boy by pointing to the logic of Scripture concerning God and how this logic left early theologians with little choice as to how to conceive of God. If the Savior is the *one* God of Israel *alone*, and the *interacting* persons of Father, Son, and Holy Spirit save, then the *one* God must exist as three eternally distinct persons! What other conclusion were the early theologians of the church able to arrive at? This was the end station determined by the place from which the train departed and by the stations that appeared on the journey from it! It also helps, I explained to her, to note that God is *one* in one way and *three* in another. God is one in *being* (or essence) and three in *person* (or relationship). She thanked me, relieved that there was a rational thought process involved in the doctrine of the Trinity after all.

Given the *personal* nature of the one God who exists eternally in three persons, impersonal examples drawn from nature are in my view of little or no value in explaining the Trinity. That an egg is distinguishable as yoke, white, and shell has no real connection with the one God in three persons. The same can be said of other examples, such as the existence of water, steam, and ice. What does this have to do with the three persons who exist as one God? What better explains the three-in-one God is a *personal* metaphor, and I think I have arrived at one, and it concerns my dog, Ringo.

Ringo is a good dog (most of the time). He is affectionate, loyal, and playful. But he doesn't have the capacity to reflect on himself in order to determine whether or not he is good. He doesn't have the power of self-reflection. But *I do*. I am able not only to behave in a way that is good, but I can contemplate what it means to be good and whether I can honestly evaluate myself as good in this way. I can also be displeased or pleased with myself. I can hate or love myself. Unlike my dog, Ringo, I have the power of self-relation. My mind can transcend or rise above myself to reflect on myself. I have this power of self-transcendence. I can creatively relate to myself, even talk to myself or be angry or happy with myself. Ringo cannot do any of these things.

Such a vast difference exists between creatures that are otherwise so similar to each other in DNA! Ringo and I are both finite or limited creatures. We are both mammals who share a kinship biologically. And yet as a self-conscious person, I am significantly more complex than he is.

Now consider this: God is *infinitely* or *limitlessly* greater and more complex than we are. Why should it be any surprise to us that the one God can relate to God's self in a way that is unimaginably complex to us? Why should we refuse to accept that God can self-relate in such a complex way that three eternally distinct agents of action or persons are involved? Given the fact that we are so significantly more complex in our capacity for self-relation than other finite mammals, why should we be baffled and shocked that an infinite mind can self-relate in ways strange or foreign to us?

Ultimately, it is the story of Jesus and not my relationship to my dog that gives us the compelling reason for believing in the Trinity! In that story, the one God of Israel who alone saves appears to save as a *loving fellowship* of Father, Son, and Holy Spirit. These three players function as this one God and Lord in the Jesus drama. No explanation is given as to why this one God who alone can save appears to save as an interaction of three. But we are stuck with the fact that these three are indeed this one God, because they all participate in the salvation of humankind, and *only* God can save!

Our God is a mystery. Seeking to understand God's complexity is like reaching for a dimension of existence beyond those with which we are aware.

> Oh, the depth of the riches of the wisdom and
> knowledge of God!
>> How unsearchable his judgments,
>> and his paths beyond tracing out!
> "Who has known the mind of the Lord?
>> Or who has been his counselor?"
> (Romans 11:33–34)

Though there is a marvelous simplicity to God, there is also an unfathomable depth of mystery.

The Lord Three Times Over

Here we are at our end station. The sign reads, "God Is a Trinity." We departed at the station that had the sign "Only God Can Save," and we have arrived at the end station, which stands for the idea that the one God and Savior is Father, Son, and Holy Spirit, an eternally interactive circle of love. Karl Barth once wrote that the Trinity is God as Lord of salvation "three times over." God is Lord of salvation as the Father, as the Son, and as the Holy Spirit.

To be the Lord of salvation is to be the only one who can save. It means that salvation comes from none other, that no one else has the capacity to save. This means that salvation is not by the works of the creature but rather by God's grace and mercy alone. The Trinity means that God is Lord of salvation at every step in the salvation process, from its origins to its fulfillment in us. As Romans 11:36 states concerning God, "For from him and through him and to him are all things." All things pertaining to salvation are from God, through God, and to God. To be more specific, all things have their origin from God the Father, come to us through the Son, Jesus Christ, and are perfected via the Holy Spirit so as to be offered back to the glory of the Father.

The Father is the Lord of salvation as the origin of all good things. James 1:17–18 says of the heavenly Father, "Every good and perfect gift is from above, coming down from the Father of the heavenly lights, who does not change like shifting shadows. He chose to give us birth through the word of truth, that we might be a kind of firstfruits of all he created." The Father willed salvation, chose that all things be redeemed by the Son, and sent the Son and the Spirit into the world to bring about salvation.

The Son, Jesus Christ, came into the world to give his life on the cross and rise again so that we could be saved (Hebrews 2:14–15; 10:5–7). The Holy Spirit assisted the Son in his act of redemption, testifies to our hearts of the good news of Christ, and then binds to Jesus those who repent and believe (Luke 4:18; John 15:26; Romans 8:9). The Spirit indwells us as the down payment of the redemption that is yet to come in the resurrection of the dead (Ephesians 1:13–14). The Spirit gradually shapes us into Christ's image and then will raise us one day from the dead so that we can bear the perfect image of Christ—for "those he justified, he also glorified" (Romans 8:30).

So, from the point of origin to the ultimate goal of perfection, salvation is the work of God and not of humanity. True, we must freely cooperate with God's grace to be saved, but the freedom to cooperate is by the very Spirit of God. Without the Spirit, we would not have the capacity to accept Christ as our Savior or to live for him (1 Corinthians 2:14). Salvation is not by works, so that no one should boast, but rather totally by the grace of God (Ephesians 2:8).

This is the meaning of the Trinity: The one God as Father, Son, and Holy Spirit is alone the Lord of salvation from beginning to end. As 1 Peter 1:2 notes, we "have been chosen according to the foreknowledge of God the Father, through the sanctifying work of the Spirit, for obedience to Jesus Christ and sprinkling by his blood."

That God is Lord of salvation three times over is the summary of our entire journey. We can imagine standing at the end station with a pair of super-powered binoculars that allows us to view the entire journey from the first station to the last. By peering into these binoculars we catch a vision of the whole and have an "Aha!" moment. The one God who alone saves is Lord of salvation three times over as Father, Son, and Holy Spirit! This means that no stage or dimension of salvation is primarily in our hands. It is all in the hands of the one God. From the eternal ordaining of salvation to its perfection in the resurrection of the dead, salvation is the work of the one Lord of all things, the triune God! This is the scriptural logic of salvation, the logic of faith concerning God's identity as Lord of salvation.

But to say that God is Lord of salvation "three times over" needs to be qualified so as to also say that all three cooperate in loving interaction in each moment of the "three times." As the Father ordains salvation as an eternal decision, the Son and the Spirit participate by willing their unique roles in this plan. As the Son obediently comes into the world as the Savior, the Father sends him and the Spirit prepares the way into flesh by anointing it for use and eventually raising the Son's body from the dead (Luke 1:35; Romans 1:4). As the Spirit is poured out to testify of the Son and to renew all of life in the Son's image, the Son continues to mediate this new life to the glory of the Father. God is Lord of salvation three times over but as a cooperation of three.

This is the full understanding of our first station, the point from which our journey began. The premise that only God can save has gone through a few stations to reach this simple but also fascinatingly complex end station, which is simply the first station more fully described. The one God who alone saves is really the Father, the Son, and the Holy Spirit. These three must be the only Savior and the only God, because *only God can save*. Salvation is not in our hands but rather in the hands of the triune God, from beginning to end.

Our next two chapters will represent a deeper exploration of the area surrounding our end station. We need to spend a little time touring this area called the Trinity. How does the Trinity enrich our understanding of salvation? This is the question we will explore next.

Study Questions:

1. Could someone proceed logically from the Old Testament teaching that God alone saves to the idea that the Father, the Son, and the Holy Spirit are three separate gods? Why or why not?

2. Can we hold that the Father, the Son, and the Holy Spirit are merely manifestations of God? Why or why not? Is this view

consistent with the stations that support the idea that the Father saves, the Son saves, and the Spirit saves? Why or why not?

3. Why is it that we find the idea of a single God who exists in three eternally distinct and interacting persons so hard to comprehend?

4. What does it mean to say that the triune God is Lord of salvation "three times over"?

5. More specifically, how do the Father, the Son, and the Holy Spirit each exercise unique lordship in salvation?

7
TOURING THE AREA
The Trinity and Salvation

We have arrived at our end station, at the doctrine of the Trinity, one God in three eternally distinct persons. We should linger here a while in order to tour the area. In particular, what is so special about it? Why was it worth coming to this place? What difference does it make that we as Christians embrace this doctrine? As I mentioned earlier, the nineteenth-century liberal theologian Friedrich Schleiermacher maintained that the classical doctrine of the Trinity was meaningless to Christian faith, and he proposed that even if the doctrine were to be eliminated, the Christian faith would not miss it. Nothing would essentially change in what we believe. I would maintain, quite to the contrary, that the Trinity structures for us the story of Jesus, so that the Christian faith calls for this doctrine and requires it. Moreover, our understanding of salvation is greatly enhanced from a more deliberate attempt to describe it with Trinitarian specificity. So, let's tour this area a bit so that we may more fully appreciate its importance to the Christian faith.

Trinitarian Structure and the Focus on Jesus Christ

The evangelical Christian movement from which I have emerged emphasizes Jesus Christ as the Savior of the world. This focus is biblical. Paul wrote that when he worked among the Corinthians he only wanted to know about "Jesus Christ and him crucified" (1 Corinthians 2:2). Though there are obviously other topics in the Bible to study, they are all in some way related to Jesus as the Savior of the world. So as we tour the town to which this final station has taken us, we need to ask if the doctrine of the Trinity somehow obscures a proper focus on Jesus as the one who died and rose again to save us. Asked another way, by noting that there are three persons involved in our salvation, do we end up demoting Jesus as the central player of his own story? Is he only one player among three and, therefore, of only limited significance to the story of redemption?

There is some validity to this line of questioning. As we noted earlier, some theologians have pointed out that in the Middle Ages the doctrine of the Trinity tended to become detached from the story of Jesus. Rather than serving to explain this drama, the doctrine of the Trinity tended to be discussed increasingly as an abstract intellectual puzzle, dealing with such issues as how God can be both three and one at the same time. This line of reasoning has validity but not at the cost of the primary need of any doctrine to somehow illuminate the story of Jesus for our time and place.

Over time, the doctrine of the Trinity has tended to obscure the central drama of our faith (the story of Jesus) rather than to highlight and explain it. This is why Schleiermacher could say that if the doctrine of the Trinity were to disappear tomorrow, no one would miss it. More recent Trinitarian theology, however, has attempted to return attention to the story of Jesus as the fundamental reason why we believe in God as triune. This trend is sometimes called the recent renewal of Trinitarian theology. We are rediscovering its value once again.

As we have shown, the story of Jesus has a Trinitarian structure. The entire story of Jesus highlights Jesus as the Son working cooperatively in loving communion with his heavenly Father and with the Holy Spirit given to him by the Father. This is not to deny that this story has its focus on Jesus. Acts 4:12 notes that there is no other name by which we are saved except that of Jesus Christ. Indeed, the name *Jesus* means "God saves" (Matthew 1:21). Our basic premise that God alone saves is indeed the meaning of Jesus' name! I come from a church background that stresses the name of Jesus as the key to experiencing all of the blessings of the gospel. We are saved by calling on the name of Jesus (Romans 10:13) and healed as we pray in that name (Acts 4:10). Moreover, baptism is cherished by some "in the name of Jesus Christ for the forgiveness" of sins (Acts 2:38). Indeed, we are washed, justified, and sanctified "in the name of the Lord Jesus Christ and by the Spirit of our God" (1 Corinthians 6:11).

Yet it is also important to note that Jesus urges us to baptize in the name of the Father, the Son, and the Holy Spirit (Matthew 28:19). Why? The reason can be found in Jesus' own baptism, where he received the Holy Spirit as the expression of his Father's love for him (Matthew 3:16–17). Jesus' baptism featured the Father's showing love to the Son through the Spirit. Jesus' own baptism was the place where the triune God was revealed for the first time in a public event. Here's the point: if we explore the actual story of how Jesus fulfilled the meaning of his name ("God saves"), we find that the God who saves in this story is actually Father, Son, and Holy Spirit.

In other words, Jesus saves precisely as the Son of the heavenly Father and as the one anointed of the Holy Spirit from the heavenly Father. Our baptism into Christ may indeed honor the name of Jesus, but to fully honor that name, we need to mention the Father, the Son, and the Holy Spirit! Indeed, the name of Jesus should more specifically mean "Father, Son, and Holy Spirit saves!" Baptism in Jesus' name should also be baptism in the name of the Father, Son, and Holy Spirit. These two baptismal formulas do not contradict each other; they are complementary.

The name of Jesus has a Trinitarian background and framework to it. As we noted earlier, the conception, baptism, death, resurrection, and ascension of Jesus are Trinitarian in framework. All of these key points in the story of Jesus originate in the Father and are performed through Jesus by means of the Holy Spirit. As we noted earlier, this is true of Jesus' conception (Luke 1:35), baptism (Matthew 3:16–17), death (Romans 8:32; Hebrews 9:14), resurrection (Romans 1:4), and ascension (Acts 2:33). We cannot focus on Jesus and what he has done for us without the Trinity. Jesus' name is a name that only has meaning within the larger framework of Jesus' relationship to his heavenly Father and with the Holy Spirit whom the Father has given him. How can the Christian faith that centers on Jesus ignore this Trinitarian framework? How can Christians do all things in Jesus' name while neglecting the Trinity? Saying, as Schleiermacher did, that we can eliminate the Trinity from Christian faith without missing it is made impossible by the very foundational narrative of our faith, namely the story of Jesus.

The same thing can be said of the name *Christ*, which literally means "anointed one." It obviously hearkens to the Father's anointing Jesus by the Holy Spirit. This anointing began at Jesus' conception in Mary's womb (Luke 1:35) and was decisively enacted at Jesus' baptism (Matthew 3:16–17). It found its fulfillment in Jesus' resurrection

(Romans 1:4) and ascension (Acts 2:33) by the agency of the Spirit. So the name *Christ* also has a Trinitarian framework. It refers to Jesus as the one anointed by the Father with the Holy Spirit. The name *Jesus Christ* can only be explained by looking at the Trinitarian involvement of God in the salvation of humanity. If there is no other name by which we are saved than Jesus Christ, then there are also no other names within which to understand Jesus Christ except Father, Son, and Holy Spirit, the names of the triune God.

The Communal God

I remember vividly my earliest view of God. I was only a kindergartner when I lay one late afternoon on the lawn of our front yard staring up into the sky. It was a perfect summer day (relatively rare in the Midwest). The sky was blue and the sun was shining brightly. It was warm with a cool breeze that kept it from becoming uncomfortable. I recall staring up at the clouds and imagining a variety of forms. One stood out: a muscular old man with a long grey beard, riding on a chariot. "This must be what God is like," I thought. "He must be stern and intolerant of evil, ready to smite the unrepentant sinners." I remember thinking, "What about me? Why am I not smitten?" I was fond of watching the Alfred Hitchcock series on television, though it frightened me greatly. I somehow became convinced that Hitchcock was the devil himself. Surely, I needed a loving God to save me from him!

As I grew older, I began to answer the question concerning my survival from wrath by focusing on what Jesus had done for me on the cross. "This is why I'm not smitten," I thought. "Jesus died so as to assuage God's wrath towards me." In my adolescent view of God, the Father and Jesus functioned like a bad cop, good cop. The Father was ready to smite me for my sins, but Jesus came along to promise me hope if I would only repent and accept him as my Savior, accept his death on the cross for me. As for the Holy Spirit, well, the Spirit was my reward for accepting Christ. The Spirit flooded into me to bring me all of the benefits of accepting Christ. What the Father had to do with all of this was relatively unclear to me.

It was only as I began to study theology that I realized what I had missed all along. First, my early leanings were implicitly tritheistic (believing in three separate gods that act independently of each other), for I had missed the unity of action involved in the one God who acts as three. I had missed the fact that it was the Father's love for the world (love for *me*) that sent Jesus and the Holy Spirit into the world to save sinners (John 3:16; Luke 15). I had missed the fact that God is essentially an inseparable and unbreakable circle of love, an intimate communion that opens itself up to include me, to include all of us.

The God who saves us, the God of the story of Jesus, is not a solitary ego who reigns on high, acting on the world while being unaffected by it. This classical view of God, influenced as it was by Greek philosophy, is not true to the biblical message, for God loves the world, is injured by people's unfaithfulness, and reaches out in suffering love to redeem. The Bible says that during the time of Noah when humanity was filled with sin, "the LORD was grieved that he had made man on the earth, and his heart was filled with pain" (Genesis 6:6). Of course, God did not give up on humanity, granting them a chance to be saved by boarding Noah's ark. But at the moment of viewing the extent of human sin, God was "filled with pain," so much so that God was momentarily flooded with regret. Much later, God had the prophet Hosea marry an unfaithful woman so that he would know what God felt like pursuing unfaithful Israel. God used judgment to block Israel's effort to pursue false gods and spoke tenderly to her in the wilderness where God had brought her for this very purpose (Hosea 2).

Of course, God is sovereign and does indeed reign from heaven over the entire cosmos. The book of Revelation, for example, shows us how wonderful it is to look above and beyond a world filled with evil and violence to see that God is indeed on the throne working out the divine plan for history, using even resistance to that plan to bring it about (see also Romans 11). Indeed, God's judgments are righteous and true (Revelation 16:7). Yet the Scriptures also say that God is love (1 John 4:8). God's sovereignty ultimately depicts the victory and reign of *divine love* over all things. Even God's judgment is motivated by love for humanity. God hates sin because God loves us so much and knows what sin does to us (it separates us from God and all that is good and just). John 3:16–17 tells us that God did not send Jesus into the world to condemn it but to save it. Then John 3:19 states that God's verdict or judgment is self-imposed by humanity: we are alienated from God because of our willful love of darkness over light.

(handwritten margin note: God sent Jesus ↓ Jesus sent the Holy Spirit ↓ Holy Spirit leads us to God + Christ)

The same point is made in Romans 1:24–28 where we are told three times that God delivered humans over to their own sinful and distorted ways. This is the wrath spoken of in Romans 1:18. It is the self-imposed alienation from the Creator caused by human sin and idolatry. But notice that God also "delivered over" his own Son to the same judgment or alienation (Romans 4:25; 8:32). God delivered sinful humanity over to its self-willed alienation and darkness and then delivered his very own Son to the same fate on the cross so as to win these sinners back. Judgment is not meant to be the final word. In Jesus, it is clearly revealed that for God, grace is meant to be the first and final word.

This insight into God is brought to greatest clarity in the story of Jesus. This is because Jesus is the fullness of grace and truth (John 1:14), for he is the radiance of God's glory and the "exact representation of his being" (Hebrews 1:3). The God revealed in the story of Jesus loves the world to the point of giving all, even the one and only favored Son (John 3:16). In harmony with the loving Father, the Son did not come to condemn the world but to save it (John 3:17). This God seeks after the lost as a desperate widow seeks a lost coin (Luke 15:8–10) or an injured father yearns for the return of an unfaithful son (Luke 15:11–32). This is the God of love. This is the Trinitarian God.

The baptism of Jesus gives us insight into this divine love; more precisely, we gain insight into the Trinitarian specificity of exactly how love is at the very being of the God revealed in the story of Jesus. Again, at Jesus' baptism, the Father responded to the devoted Son by saying, "This is my Son, whom I love; with him I am well pleased" (Matthew 3:17). As the Father said this, the Holy Spirit was seen coming forth from the Father and resting on Jesus. The implication is that the Spirit was the expression of the Father's love for the Son. In the very next verse (Matthew 4:1), the Spirit led the Son into the desert to be tested by the Devil. Empowered by the Spirit, the Son returned devotion to the Father by being faithful in testing. So not only was the Spirit the expression of the Father's love for the Son but also the power by which the Son returned love to the Father.

Clearly, God is love because God is the Father who loves the Son, and the Son who loves the Father, and the Holy Spirit who is the essence and bond of this love as well as the one who participates in it by loving the Father and the Son, for the Spirit is God's love in action (Romans 5:5). *God is by nature a circle of love, a communion among Father, Son, and Holy Spirit. This is most clearly, most specifically what it means to say that God is love.* Yet this circle is not closed but open to us. The Son and the Spirit came forth into the world to open this divine circle to *embrace us.* As we noted earlier, the triune God worked together to offer up Jesus as our substitute on the cross so that God could meet us precisely at our darkest place of bondage, our sin and death. From there, the triune God raised Jesus from the dead and imparted the Spirit of new life to us so that we could escape our bondage and live within the embrace of Father, Son, and Spirit.

We are now prepared to show more fully how the Trinity enriches our understanding of personal salvation.

Trinitarian Salvation

When I was a child, I was prone to think that salvation was mainly about escape from hell and going to heaven when I die. If I could just "make it to heaven," all would be well! It took me years to figure out (mainly by listening more carefully to my father's sermons and then studying theology later on my own) that my understanding of salvation was distorted. In fact, it largely left God out of the picture. The only role that God played in this little escape plan of mine was in offering me the escape route to begin with. It was up to me to take advantage of it and to make my escape by following the Bible. Little did I know that salvation was actually in the loving embrace of a triune God who sought to heal me through the gift of divine love by the living presence of the divine Spirit within.

Well, most Christians may not be functioning today with the distorted idea of salvation that I had early on. But I have found that they still tend to reduce everything to forgiveness. When the average Christian thinks of salvation what usually comes to mind is the forgiveness of sins. We commonly hear that God has forgiven us of our sins and will not hold these sins against us any longer. We are therefore free from judgment; for many evangelicals this means freedom from hell. Of course, I am not denying that forgiveness is indeed a valuable aspect of salvation. The Bible says,

> "Blessed are they
>> whose transgressions are forgiven,
>> whose sins are covered.

> Blessed is the man
>> whose sin the Lord will never count against him."
> (Romans 4:7–8)

We are truly blessed to know that God has in Christ forgiven us all of our sins and that these sins remain covered by the sacrifice of Christ on our behalf. As Isaiah 53:6 states, "the Lord has laid on him [Christ] the iniquity of us all." He "took up our infirmities" (53:4). Indeed,

> He was pierced for our transgressions,
>> he was crushed for our iniquities;
> the punishment that brought us peace was upon him,
>> and by his wounds we are healed. (Isaiah 53:5)

There is no doubt that Jesus carried away our sin and its punishment so that we could be forgiven. But notice that the above text also notes that by Jesus' wounds we are "healed." This healing is not only spiritual but physical, implying that the good news of the gospel affects every avenue of life. Faith effects wholeness of life-producing *shalom*, or well-being in God, in all. I don't refer here to a guarantee of wealth or perfect health, but I do believe that the life of the Spirit leads to a deep sense of wholeness and strengthening of body and soul to fulfill the will of the Lord. And of course the goal of salvation is the resurrection from the dead. Indeed, salvation is not only forgiveness but is also *renewal*.

According to Scripture, salvation is not just forgiveness, and not even just renewal or resurrection. It has a substance that is deep and rich, namely fellowship or communion in the embrace of the triune God. When we accept Jesus as our Lord and Savior, the Spirit of God comes into our lives in an intimate relationship with us (we say that the Spirit "indwells," even "fills" us to overflowing). Romans 5:5 tells us that this entry of the Holy Spirit into us brings a rich and abundant experience of God's love into our lives. It is this love that is healing, renewing, and strengthening. This love is the victory over sin and death. Notice how Paul described the victory of God's love in granting us the everlasting and victorious life:

> Who shall separate us from the love of Christ? Shall trouble or hardship or persecution or famine or nakedness or danger or sword? As it is written: "For your sake we face death all day long; we are considered as sheep to be slaughtered." No, in all these things we are more than conquerors through him who loved us. For I am convinced that neither death nor life, neither angels nor demons, neither the present nor the future, nor any powers, neither height nor depth, nor anything else in all creation, will be able to separate us from the love of God that is in Christ Jesus our Lord. (Romans 8:35–39)

Notice that Paul locates the love poured out into our lives by the Holy Spirit as the very substance of our life with God. This is what carries us through the dark moments and keeps us going when we feel weary. This is what convinces us that salvation is real and enduring. This is what empowers us to give of ourselves in Christ's name to others. What is still needed is to look more closely at this love in the light of the story of Jesus, in the light of its Trinitarian framework.

Recall what was said above about the Trinitarian framework of the story of Jesus. In fact, the entire story of the Trinity is a love story about the bond of love in the Holy Spirit between the Father and the Son. It is an eternal story (John 17:5, 24). Picture this: from all eternity there is this bond of love (the Holy Spirit) encircling the heavenly Father and the one and only Son. The Spirit participates actively in providing this bond by loving the Father and the Son and delighting in their love for one another. The Spirit will also delight in abundantly gushing forth to share this bond of love with others, taking them into this circle of love.

Together, as one God, the three decided to create. This was a momentous decision. God was not lonely, for there was always this wonderful circle of love. But there was also this free decision to expand the circle to include others, though not because God needed to, for God was always fulfilled as God and did not need anyone else (Acts 17:25). But God freely decided to open this circle of love to others. So God created.

I have often thought that this decision to create must not have been an easy decision for God. After all, the Bible indicates that God sees the future, "the end from the beginning" (Isaiah 46:10). God knew that creating humanity would bring a lot of suffering into the creation. God knew that creating people with the freedom to sin would result in sin and suffering, for creatures as well as for the creator God. We know that God knew this, because Revelation 13:8 refers to Christ as the "Lamb that was slain from the creation of the world." In other words, from the time God created (from eternity, in fact) God knew that the one and only Son would have to suffer and die to win the creation back from its wayward path. God knew when creating that humanity would sin and bring untold suffering on everyone.

So why did God still create? Does not anything worth doing in life involve some kind of cost? When I decided to earn my doctorate at a Swiss university, I knew that this decision would involve hardship and suffering as well as many wonderful experiences. I was so right. Lacking funds and an adequate grasp of the German language, I had to work hard along with my wife to make a good life for ourselves during my demanding years of study. But the rewards made the entire journey worthwhile. Jesus himself said that anytime we want to do something worthwhile, we must count the cost (Luke 14:28). God counted the cost when deciding to create, too, and decided that it was still worth creating despite the cost in both pain and loss.

This is something about God's decision to create that we find hard to understand. Our vision of reality is overshadowed by sin and suffering, since this is the state of our existence. Though we yearn and groan inwardly for the liberty of the world to come, we only see it dimly (1 Corinthians 13:12). The glory of the coming redemption that will be a reality in the resurrection of the dead and the new heavens and new earth cannot be seen clearly by us now. Our minds could not take it in. As a result, we don't see the glorious end that God planned when he decided from all eternity to create. So it is difficult for us to grasp what motivated God to create, what made creation worth doing despite the darkness and suffering that the first humans would bring on the world. God knew the glory of end-time redemption and the glories of the journey towards that goal and decided that life was worth creating.

As noted earlier, God the Father created the world by and for Christ (Colossians 1:16). This was done by the Spirit (Genesis 1:2). In other words, the creation was made by God as a circle of love to be the dwelling place of the Spirit and the "house" of the favored Son to the glory of the Father. But when the Son became flesh and entered his household, the world did not recognize him. Not even the chosen people of God (Israel) recognized him (John 1:10–11). But God accepted as part of the divine family anyone from all peoples of the world who would accept Christ (John 1:12). The entire story of Jesus takes place as the Son succeeds with the aid of the Spirit in witnessing to the Father's love for the world and in winning it back (John 3:16–18). The world crucified Jesus as a blasphemer cursed of God. Ironically, it was the act of crucifixion itself that was the act of blasphemy. Rather than being the place where Jesus was cursed of God, the cross was more accurately the place where God placed on

Jesus the weight of the human curse due to their sin and rejection of God:

> Surely he took up our infirmities,
>> and carried our sorrows,
>> yet we considered him stricken by God,
>> smitten by him, and afflicted.
> But he was pierced for our transgressions,
>> he was crushed for our iniquities;
>> the punishment that brought us peace was upon him,
>> and by his wounds we are healed. (Isaiah 53:4–5)

The Father suffered by offering up the Son to the cross and the Son suffered in offering himself in obedience to the Father. The Spirit was there on the cross, having led the Son there in love for humanity. The Spirit suffered as the love extended to humanity was rejected, being blasphemed in this rejection.

But in the death and resurrection of Jesus, the love of God conquered human sin and rejection; death itself was overcome. The Father raised the Son by the power of the Spirit as the favored Son and as the doorway for human salvation. The divine love is all-powerful, having a limitless capacity to suffer. No amount of human sin and suffering can overwhelm God and conquer this divine love. The resurrection is proof of the limitless capacity of God as a circle of love to bear all things in offering grace to the lost. This is why Paul was so convinced in Romans 8:35–39 that nothing can separate us from this love, not even death itself.

The entire story of Jesus is a story of how God as a circle of love opened up to receive sinful and bruised humanity in order to heal and redeem it. When Jesus prayed the Lord's Prayer, he prayed, "*Our* Father." Jesus was the one and only Son (John 3:16). He was the only one who had the right to address the heavenly Father as "Father."

Yet Jesus did not pray, "*My* Father," (which was his right) but rather, "*Our* Father" (Matthew 6:9). His praying, "Our Father," was an act of grace. He was including us! He was allowing us to enter into his circle of love with the heavenly Father and to call *his* Father *our* Father.

By the Holy Spirit, we are drawn to Christ as our Savior. If we accept Christ, we become members of his body through the Spirit as a bond of love and have deep communion with Christ. By bearing the Holy Spirit, as the bond of love between the Son and the Father, we are allowed to participate in Jesus' sonship, in his love relationship with the heavenly Father. Our communion with Christ through the Holy Spirit becomes the open door to the communion with the heavenly Father that Christ enjoys. As sons and daughters of God in Christ, we gain through the Spirit all of the benefits of Jesus' relationship with the heavenly Father. "We in Christ" and "Christ in us" mean that *we are in the circle of love between the Father and the Son, and that they are in us*. This is what Jesus planned on his way to the cross, praying to the heavenly Father, "Father, . . . you are in me and I am in you. May they also be in us so that the world may believe that you have sent me" (John 17:21).

The doctrine of the Trinity enriches our understanding of salvation. It shows us that salvation is not primarily about escaping hell or having our guilt relieved. Salvation is being rescued and healed by the loving embrace of the Father, the Son, and the Holy Spirit. Salvation is about deliverance from the alienation of sin and death for communion with God and all of the blessings that go with this. Trinitarian salvation is communion. It calls us out of our self-centered existence to the embrace of another, the circle of love that we come to know as the loving embrace of Father, Son, and Holy Spirit. This embrace focuses on Jesus, on becoming adopted into his body and into his sonship. We receive this adoption by placing our faith in Jesus and by receiving his Holy Spirit, the Spirit that rested on him and that he poured forth on us from his heavenly Father. This is the Spirit that allows us to cry out through Jesus to the Father as our Father and that testifies to our spirits that we are indeed participants in Jesus' sonship. This is the Spirit that will one day raise us from the dead in a way similar to Jesus' resurrection so that we can be fully filled with the Spirit of life in the image of Jesus. At this conclusion of our salvation, we will be fully incorporated into the loving communion of Father, Son, and Holy Spirit. Now we see God only dimly but then "face to face" (1 Corinthians 13:12).

Trinitarian Salvation and Human Fulfillment

Salvation as communion is a richer notion of salvation than mere forgiveness of sins. Forgiveness is indeed a valuable component of salvation in the context of Trinitarian communion, but by itself it is insufficient to describe the rich texture of salvation according to the New Testament. As Jesus prayed to his heavenly Father, "Just as you are in me and I am in you. May they also be in us so that the world may believe that you have sent me" (John 17:21).

This richer understanding of salvation that the Trinitarian doctrine allows also answers a deep-seated need within us to be healed relationally. We are, after all, relational beings through and through. Even within our mothers' wombs we are already dependent on another, relating to another, cradled within the embrace of another, even if it be a womb. After birth, we relate to significant care persons and bond with them. Our sense of self is formed in relation to them. Eventually, we consciously form our sense of self from their facial expressions and acts of caring.

We then develop a sense of self within an ever-expanding and increasingly complex web of relationships. Who am I? I am a husband, a father, a son, a friend, a brother, a professor, a pastor, and a neighbor—all of which depict relational realities. I cannot possibly define myself apart from this web of relationships. As the famous philosopher Martin Buber once maintained, relation is an "ontological" reality, meaning that relation is essential to who we are as human beings. Buber even wrote in *I and Thou*, "In the beginning is the relation," an obvious play on the opening words of Genesis. He meant by this that we are made to be relational beings. He was right about this.

The Genesis creation account is clear on this point. Humanity was not created as a solitary person but rather as a partnership, a relation of two, man and woman. Both together made up the image of God in humanity (Genesis 1:27). By partnering in mutual love and respect to procreate and to exercise responsible stewardship or lordship over the earth, they would image God as the loving Creator and author of life (Genesis 1:28), the God who spoke in the first person plural, "Let us make man in our image" (Genesis 1:26). The relational God creates relational humans to mimic God in the context of just and loving relationships. This is what theologians call in Latin the *analogia amoris*, the analogy (or similarity) of love that exists between humanity and God (also called the *analogia relationis*, the analogy of relation between humanity and God).

The second creation narrative, which we have in Genesis 2, elaborates on the relationality of human nature. Genesis 1 repeatedly notes that the creation that God made was regarded by God as "good" at every stage (e.g., Genesis 1:10). All of a sudden, the narrative comes to a screeching halt at the creation of a solitary human. God noted that it was "not good" for such a solitary being to exist (Genesis 2:18). In a sense, the first human, Adam, was not really alone, for there were animals all around him. But in another sense Adam *was* alone for there was no one to be an equal, no one to share God's image with as a self-conscious being. So God made a partner for Adam from his flesh and bone, and called her Eve.

Some think that before the creation of Eve, the first human was genderless. It was with the creation of Eve that God divided humanity into male and female, the first human becoming male and the second female. Regardless of whether this view is correct, the point is that the first human was alone because there was no human partner to share the image of God with, as depicted in Genesis 1:27–28. Humanity was created as a relational being. The relational God (as a circle of love) created a relational being to mimic that love and partnership in life.

Circle of love = Trinity

This is not to deny that we are individuals who need to resist being bound by the expectations of others. As Carl Jung noted in his classic *The Undiscovered Self,* we are not to lose ourselves in the corporate "spirit." But neither are we to alienate ourselves from others as though we were islands. Sin means that our relational reality is distorted, plagued by the threat of alienation from others as well as the threat of assimilation to the unjust expectations of others. We yearn for redemption, for a liberated existence within a web of loving and just relationships. We yearn for the communion of the triune God, and within God, the communion of saints. The relational, Trinitarian God answers our deepest need for salvation and provides a richly relational salvation that is alone adequate to truly save "to the uttermost."

Study Questions:

1. How did the doctrine of the Trinity in the Middle Ages obscure the story of Jesus? What have Trinitarian theologians done recently to reverse this trend?

2. Explain the Trinitarian structure of the name of Jesus.

3. Explain the Trinitarian structure of the name of Christ.

4. What is wrath or judgment in the light of the God of love?

5. Use the example of Jesus' baptism to show with Trinitarian specificity how God is love.

6. How does the "Our Father" of Jesus' Lord's Prayer point us in the direction of Trinitarian salvation?

7. Why does Trinitarian salvation fulfill our deepest needs as beings made to bear God's image?

8. In general, according to this chapter, how can the doctrine of the Trinity enrich our understanding of salvation?

8
POSTCARDS TO THE WORLD
Trinitarian Practice

Our trip has taken us to the station that refers to the one God who exists as an interactive circle of love consisting of Father, Son, and Holy Spirit. We have toured the area to see what this doctrine says about God's identity as the Savior. God saves as an interactive fellowship of Father, Son, and Holy Spirit. We also saw how the Trinity enhances our understanding of salvation. As we noted, salvation is not just forgiveness of sins but is a divine embrace into which people of faith are drawn. More specifically, we are drawn by the Holy Spirit into communion with Christ and through Christ into communion with his heavenly Father. In other words, by the Spirit that anointed Jesus as the divine Son and raised him from the dead, we are anointed with this very same sonship (and daughtership) so that we can enjoy all of its benefits: communion with the heavenly Father and life everlasting, including resurrection in the very image of Christ. The Holy Spirit within testifies with our spirits that we are children of God, the same

Spirit by which we cry "Abba! Father!" and await the full adoption that will occur in the resurrection (Romans 8:15–23).

The question that we wish to ask in this final chapter is, "So what?" What does the Trinity have to do with Christian life and practice? How does it affect our worship and witness? Most trips include postcards sent to family and friends. We do this to testify to others of the great time that we are having. Trinitarian life involves postcards, too, namely our witness sent not only to friends and family but to the world!

Trinitarian Worship

I sat in the little hut of a man who had kindly taken me in during my long drive across the country to return to Vanguard University to complete my senior year in college. I had reached California and was passing through Fresno when I discovered that I needed a place to bunk for the night. He had been introduced to me by a mutual friend and had graciously invited me to stay with him for the night. He shared a humble meal with me and then took the opportunity to ask some theological questions that had been on his mind for quite some time. He knew that I was a religion major and wanted to know what I thought about matters that meant a lot to him.

His major question had to do with worship. He noted that worship for him was very personal, quite meaningful and rich whenever he was alone with God. But as soon as he went to church, things seemed to change. He found it awkward and even exhausting to worship with others according to a planned order of service. I then asked him if it would be possible to bring his personal experience with God into the public service so as to inspire others with it. He had this wonderful experience with God taking place in private worship; he just needed to take this with him into the corporate worship setting so that others might be inspired to seek the same.

Of course, neither of us wanted to use worship in order to show off spiritually in front of others. Jesus condemned such spiritual showmanship (Matthew 6:18). But passionate and sincere worship in a corporate setting tends to be contagious. It helps to provide an atmosphere that inspires others to yield to God in worship as well. The thought that corporate worship has this dual dimension of glorifying God and encouraging others was a thought that had not occurred to my new friend. I explained to him that worship can be passionate and real because we do not do it in our own strength. Worship is an act of letting go of those things we cling to and yielding to a pull coming from the Holy Spirit who dwells within. By the Spirit we share in the communion that is enjoyed among the persons of the Godhead, a sharing that is mimicked in our fellowship among one another.

This is the point: If the triune God is an open fellowship of persons that transforms us, then we who are transformed by God should become a people who are open to fellowship with others. The fellowshipping God gives rise to a fellowshipping people. There should be an impulse deep within us not to confine worship to the private prayer closet, as important as this is. This impulse should drive us outward to embrace others as this triune God has embraced us. It should help us to realize that all things spiritual have divine love at their essence and have a corporate dimension to them. Elements of the spiritual life are not fulfilled in us until we reach out to experience them in communion with others.

As Ephesians 3:18 notes, we grasp the richness of God's love "with all the saints." There is little wonder that when Paul talked about the church he commonly did so in the context of a reference to God as triune (Ephesians 4:3–6; 1 Corinthians 12:4–6). We simply cannot

Church

say that we love God while hating others, for "whoever does not love does not know God, because God is love" (1 John 4:8).

Life lived in the love of God as Trinity actually begins in adoration or worship. Before we ever think of the Trinity as an intellectual issue we participate in the Trinity through praise and adoration. We share together in worship the wonderful communion enjoyed among the persons of the Godhead. In fact, the Eastern churches have always insisted on this very point, namely that the belief in the Trinity begins in worship. We adore the heavenly Father through the Son and by the power of the Holy Spirit. Or, we adore the Son to the ultimate glory of the Father and by the power of the Holy Spirit. Or, we invoke the Spirit among us to adore the Spirit and to worship the Son to the glory of the Father or to worship the Father through the Son. There is a wonderful variety and also a consistent structure to Trinitarian worship.

Indeed, the precise function of the triune God in worship varies, though it also has a kind of consistency to it. It varies because our relationship with God involves a multifaceted circle of love. We turn to the Father or to the Son or to the Holy Spirit in worship. We enjoy this wonderful variety. Yet the function of the Trinity in worship is consistent because the story of Jesus that informs our faith defines the functions of Father, Son, and Holy Spirit very precisely. The Father sends the Son and the Holy Spirit into the world to save it, the Son is sent by the Father to become flesh under the anointing of the Spirit, and the Spirit is sent by the Father to rest on the incarnate Son and to be poured forth on us through the Son.

The Bible does not confuse these very precise roles. For example, the Son does not send the Father into the world to become flesh, and the Spirit is not sent by the Father into the world to become flesh. Only the Son is sent to become flesh. The Father sends and the Spirit anoints or indwells; only the Son becomes flesh (John 1:14, see also 1:18). Since there is a consistency in the story of Jesus and to the entire New Testament with regard to the functions of the Father, the Son, and the Holy Spirit, there is also a consistency to how the Trinity functions in Christian worship.

Since the heavenly Father sent the Son and the Spirit into the world to save us, and all things will be fulfilled at the end of time when the Son and the Spirit restore creation to the Father (1 Corinthians 15:24), worship recognizes the Father as the one who is ultimately the source of all things and the one to whom all glory is ultimately given. So even though all glory goes to the Son, we have in our songs and prayers (or at least in the back of our minds) that this glory given to the Son is to the ultimate glory of the heavenly Father who sent the Son to save us.

Similarly, since the Holy Spirit is sent to us through the Son so that we may testify of the Son and be shaped in the Son's image, we invoke and glorify the Spirit as we glorify the Son and the heavenly Father through him. So there is a rich variety to how the triune God is worshiped and prayed to, and there is also a consistent pattern that is faithful to the functions assigned to the persons of the Godhead in the story of Jesus.

Our worship leaders and those who write our songs or revise our liturgies and prayers attempt to orchestrate worship so that it remains faithful to the functions attributed to the persons of the triune God in the story of Jesus. But there is no question that confusion has arisen from a lack of knowledge in this area. A student of mine (Susan Hammond) recently wrote a master's thesis analyzing the songs popularly sung in evangelical worship services. She showed that there is no small degree of confusion about the roles assigned to the persons of the Trinity in these songs. For example, some of them refer to Jesus as our heavenly Father!

It is also important to note that a prayer spoken or a song sung to one person of the Godhead is given to *all* of God and not to a *part* of

God. God does not have parts! The Trinity is not three separate gods. Each person of the Trinity functions as *God*; each one does this, as well as the three in communion. Also, when one person of the Godhead acts or receives glory, the other two are not sleeping or on vacation! The three persons are inseparable, since they subsist within the one God and share the one essence of deity.

So something sung to one person of the Godhead goes to God and implicitly involves the other two persons as well. Yet highlighting one person in worship has meaning also, since each person of the Godhead carries a unique point of emphasis in the corporate work of the triune God. For example, though all three persons participate in every work of the one God, the Father is uniquely designated the Creator, the Son the Redeemer, and the Holy Spirit the Giver of life—the one who perfects the redemption wrought by the Son.

Since the triune God is a circle of love, all worship takes place within the divine embrace. We embrace the God who is already embracing us. All worship is a return embrace to a loving God who has opened the divine life to embrace us in our sin and death in order to forgive and to heal us. This God has opened up to being wounded by us in embracing us. In worship, we show thanksgiving and praise to this God for opening up to us, embracing, forgiving, and healing us. We also express hope for the future that this divine embrace has opened to us. All of this takes place *to* God and also *within* God. The Trinity means that our worship is not to a distant deity who resides above the clouds but to a God who is also near. In fact, we worship within this God, within the divine embrace.

Also keep in mind that the heavenly Father glorified the Son by loving the Son before the worlds were made, from all eternity (John 17:5, 24). The Son also glorifies the heavenly Father as the Father glorifies him: "Father, the time has come. Glorify your Son, that your Son may glorify you" (John 17:1). The Holy Spirit also glorifies them both in being the bond of love between them. It is by the Spirit that we glorify Jesus as Lord (1 Corinthians 12:3), which is to the ultimate glory of the Father (Philippians 2:11). The persons of the Trinity glorify each other in loving one another. In worship believers get pulled into this circle of glory, this circle of love. By the Holy Spirit we glorify Jesus, and through Jesus, our heavenly Father. *We have the privilege in worship of participating in a circle of divine glory and love that has existed from all eternity.*

This worship further transforms us from self-centered creatures to persons who discover greater and greater liberty to yield to God in giving God glory. We cannot be self-centered and be sincerely yielding to the impulse of the Holy Spirit to glorify God at the same time. Sin is self-centered and therefore falls terribly short of God's wonderful glory (Romans 3:23). In contrast, worship is the enjoyment of the capacity to glorify God granted to us through Jesus' death and resurrection and the gift of the Holy Spirit within. By yielding to the Spirit's work and letting go of our self-centered concerns, we find the liberty to praise God for God's own sake within God's loving embrace. This is the reason we were created; this is the true reason for life itself. In this worship we taste the freedom granted to us in the gospel.

This yielding to God also helps to bridge belief and life. The best way to really begin to live what we believe is to first worship in a way that is true to what we believe. If beliefs do not find deep root in our hearts through worship, they will hardly find powerful expression in life. Conversely, if core values and beliefs are not lived out, our worship will tend to lack credibility. But in this case, the worship is questionable in its genuineness. The bridge to life is best paved through genuine worship in which people submit together to God, to one another in Jesus' name, and to God's will for the world. As our beliefs find expression within the liberty of worship, they will also find greater expression within the liberated life. The witness of that liberated life will then add credibility to our worship. People will not think that our worship is insincere if they see us loving or caring for others.

Trinitarian Witness

Trinitarian worship leads to Trinitarian witness. Worship takes place "in Spirit and truth" (John 4:24). Worship itself bears witness to the truth of Christ in the Holy Spirit to the glory of the Father. There is no worship that is not supported by the truth and does not live from the truth of Christ. This is in part the link between Trinitarian worship and Trinitarian witness to truth.

Yet witness also spills out beyond the sacred space of worship to invite others to the banquet table of fellowship and ministry. Of course, witness continues to glorify God. We seek to glorify God in all that we do. Like worship, witness is also an intratrinitarian reality. The Father witnesses for the Son (John 8:18), just as the Son witnesses for the Father (John 1:18). The Holy Spirit comes from the Father to bear witness to the Son (John 15:26). The Son also points to the Spirit as the one who will lead the disciples into all truth (John 16:13). The persons of the Trinity witness to one another of the truth of the one God. There is also a dominant pattern to this witness. The Father bears witness to the Son through the Spirit while the Spirit bears witness to the Son on behalf of the Father.

When we receive the Holy Spirit, we gain the capacity to become witnesses to the Son on behalf of the heavenly Father. Jesus said to his disciples, "You will receive power when the Holy Spirit comes on you; and you will be my witnesses" (Acts 1:8). We witness to Jesus before the world that he is indeed the Son of the living God and the path to salvation. The world has condemned and rejected Christ as the Son of the living God but God vindicated him by raising him from the dead by the agency of the Spirit. Jesus was proclaimed the Son of

God through resurrection (Romans 1:4). We now witness to Jesus as God's Son as well, by the Spirit alive in us. We witness of God's love for humanity manifested in Christ and made real within the hearts of those who believe.

We are drawn in by faith to the life of the Spirit and to the Spirit's witness to the Son on behalf of the heavenly Father. Witness is not just something we *do*; it is first something we *are*. Jesus said that his followers would *be* his witnesses once the Spirit came within (Acts 1:8). Our lives together as the people of God bear witness to the love of God present in the embrace of the triune God.

In Acts 2 the church was filled with the Holy Spirit to be witnesses to Jesus on behalf of the heavenly Father. The church did this not only by proclaiming the good news but also in the richness of their shared fellowship (Acts 2:42), their sharing goods with those in need (2:45), and their breaking bread together in one another's homes with glad and thankful hearts (2:46). The result was that "the Lord added to their number daily those who were being saved" (2:47). The witness is in life as well as in words. The witness takes place within the loving embrace of the triune God and participates in the loving witness of the persons of the Godhead to one another.

The Gospel of John records Jesus' prayer to the heavenly Father that the disciples be one "so that the world may believe" (John 17:21). Notice again how the quality of their shared life bears witness to Jesus. This oneness of the people of God is a rich fellowship in which the people of God share life together just as the Father and the Son do through the power of the Spirit. This is done as God's people are "in God," that is, incorporated into the loving communion and mutual witness of the Father and the Son. Notice Jesus' words: "I pray . . . that all of them may be one, Father, just as you are in me and I am in you. May they also be in us so that the world may believe that you have sent me" (17:20–21).

I recall recently being invited as a guest speaker to a small church located not far from my home town. These kind people had recently decreased in number and were feeling the pressure from the subsequent decline in funds and resources. I spoke to them from Acts 2 about the quality of life shared among the earliest followers of Jesus. I then noted that these people in the book of Acts broke bread in one another's homes in small groups with glad and sincere hearts. They shared life freely together and took care of those in need, which was attractive to those who came across their movement. The point that struck me, I explained, was that this quality of life that they had together did not require a lot of people, and neither did it require resources and talent. What drove it was the gift of the Holy Spirit and the Spirit's devoted witness to the heavenly Father and to the one and only Son. The key to "success" in the church is the life of the triune God. Best of all, this life is free and available to groups of any size! All that we have to do is to let go of our discouragement and self-preoccupations and yield to the leading of the Holy Spirit!

People who participate in the life of the triune God must be convinced of its value. To convince us, the Holy Spirit also bears witness to our spirits that we are the children of God (Romans 8:15–16). This witness is needed because we are inherently weak; our redemption is not yet fulfilled. Though we are born again and made new creatures in Christ with God's Spirit residing within, we still live in this mortal body that is subject to weakness, sin, and death. Under the burden of this flesh, we still groan within for the liberty of the future resurrection of the dead, knowing that our adoption as people of the Holy Spirit and as brothers and sisters of Jesus will only be fulfilled at that time (Romans 8:23; 2 Corinthians 5:1–5). We are still subject to weakness and doubt as we live by faith and not by sight. For this reason, the Holy Spirit continues to bear witness to our spirits within that we are indeed God's children, people of the Spirit and brothers and sisters of

Jesus within the love of his Father. All other voices are silenced as we cling to this one voice of the Spirit. No other voice matters but this one.

It is from the strength of this inner voice of the Holy Spirit that we witness to others of the possibility of becoming God's children and joining the family of God at that banquet table of the Lord. We must first become convinced of our own place at the table of the family of God before we can invite others to come. This is especially true if we intend to invite others with real conviction. The strength of our witness will not come through "mind over matter" but rather from our growth in the inner witness of the Holy Spirit to our shared sonship with Jesus Christ as his brothers and sisters. Our witness to Christ in the power of the Spirit grows stronger as we grow in the reality of this divine embrace of our lives within the life of the triune God.

We must keep in mind that the success of our witness is not ultimately in our hands but rather in the hands of the triune God. Of course, we must grow in dedication, wisdom, and love in order to become more effective witnesses. There is also a place for a disciplined studying of the Bible and Christian theology to gain a clearer understanding of the truth and its relevance to others. But ultimately, God is the one who speaks to the hearts of those we speak to. God is the one who causes the new song of the gospel to penetrate our hearts and to be played through us (Ephesians 5:18–19). We should seek to become more effective instruments, and we also need to recognize that it remains the triune God who plays the music and effects the hearing in others.

Trinitarian Ethics

Trinitarian life begins in the fellowship of the triune God. It begins in the loving embrace and communion of Father, Son, and

Holy Spirit. The witness effected by this love and communion not only leads us to point to Jesus and to the heavenly Father as the source of all life and love but also causes us to deal with others and with the entire environment with justice and mercy. In other words, we are called to treat others in a way that is consistent with the kingdom of God.

What is the kingdom of God? Briefly put, the kingdom of God is the sovereign reign of the triune God in the world. This reign is not far away but near and transformative. The kingdom is not a place but rather a *presence*. It concerns the presence of the triune God that was opened to us in the coming of Christ and the Holy Spirit. God's presence overthrows the dark powers and establishes God's liberating reign in people's lives and in all of creation. As Jesus said in Matthew 12:28, "If I drive out demons by the Spirit of God, then the kingdom of God has come upon you." The kingdom of God comes on us in power to draw us into God's liberating reign and to bring us under God's lordship in all things. In fulfilling God's lordship, the kingdom of God fulfills the will of the Father and is inaugurated in creation by Jesus Christ, God's only Son, in cooperation with the Holy Spirit. As Jesus said, the reign of God in fulfilling the Father's will came on people as a source of liberation through the presence of the Holy Spirit. As we receive the Spirit by believing on Jesus, we participate in the freedom to live for God within God's kingdom.

Living under God's reign or lordship implies that we value those things that God values and that we obey God's laws with heart as well as with mind and deed. Jesus asks us to seek first the kingdom of God and its righteousness, and all things that we are legitimately concerned about will be added to us (Matthew 6:33). All of Jesus' teachings imply that he is describing right living under God's lordship or reign. All of Jesus' teachings seek to guide a life in faithfulness to the heavenly Father according to the example of Jesus and within the freedom that Jesus and the work of the Holy Spirit provide. Let us look at several of the main lines of these teachings.

Jesus places love—the love that he shares with the heavenly Father via the work of the Holy Spirit (Matthew 3:16–17)—as essential to life that is free and faithful to God. The doctrine of the Trinity means that God is not a solitary ego but an interactive circle of love. The God of the kingdom is the God of love. Love reigns over history and God's creation. Hate, greed, and violence will not reign over all things but rather love, justice, and peace. This is what God stands for and this is what those who live within God's kingdom yearn, pray, and work for. The triune God reigns through the interactive circle of love that constitutes the one God of Scripture.

Jesus places this love and justice at the very base of obedience to God's law. Love is expressed in mutual care and concern for others, while justice extends mutual respect and dignity, allowing others to have the opportunity to be all that God has willed for them to be. This love and justice are precisely what the Old Testament affirms. Deuteronomy introduces the importance of obeying the commandments by claiming that God is one and that ultimate love and devotion belongs, therefore, to this God alone: "Hear, O Israel: The LORD our God, the LORD is one. Love the LORD your God with all your heart and with all your soul and with all your strength" (Deuteronomy 6:4–5). Then the challenge of obeying the commandments is given in the very next verse (Deuteronomy 6:6). Similarly, Amos criticized Israel for engaging in ceremonial worship but neglecting justice and mercy among one another. Amos recorded God as saying to Israel:

> Away with the noise of your songs!
> I will not listen to the music of your harps.

> But let justice roll on like a river,
>
> righteousness like a never-failing stream!
>
> (Amos 5:23–24)

Amos made it clear that love and justice, and not ceremony, are at the foundation of the law.

Jesus in fact criticized the Jewish leaders for placing religious ceremony and other less important ordinances above the core values of the law such as justice, mercy, and faithfulness (Matthew 23:23). In Matthew 5, Jesus told his followers that their entry one day into the fulfillment of the kingdom of God on earth assumes a righteousness that exceeds that of these leaders (Matthew 5:20). Our righteousness transcends that of these leaders if it begins with love and devotion towards God and justice, rather than towards less important matters of religious ceremony and social standing in the community.

These priorities of the kingdom of God became clear to me when I was growing up in the Pentecostal church of my youth. The majority of the inner core of the church attended church regularly, sang the hymns, and gave to the offering plate. These were all very worthy things to do. Yet the thing that really stayed with me when I left home for college was the love that I observed among these people. It was not the attendance roll or the amount of money that the church took in that made a lasting impression on me. This was not the legacy that I carried with me when I left town to become a responsible Christian adult. It was the examples of sacrificial love for others that I had observed among them that impacted me. It reminds me of what Jesus said when he stated that our righteousness must transcend practices of religious ceremony to address issues of human compassion and mercy.

I also noticed, however, that not many at the small Bible college I attended talked much about the great issues facing the world. These were sincere and godly people in many ways but social issues were not hot topics on campus among the general student population. It was 1970 and some on campus were concerned about Vietnam, pollution, and civil rights. Yet we rarely talked about such things. Surely the love and justice of the kingdom of God had something to offer us in our reflection on such issues. Interpersonal love goes a long way, but the Bible also has something to say about far-away people, strangers, systems of power, and the care of creation. For example, the law talks about not killing, deceiving, or dealing with our neighbors unjustly. If we ignore such things, we run the risk of advocating a "cheap" or easy grace that makes no demands on us. Grace is free, but it demands everything in return among those who receive it.

Yet it is important to stress also that we are embraced by the triune God "just as we are," as sinners; we cannot earn our salvation. Since love within the divine embrace of the Trinity is the beginning of the law, it compels us to reject the legalistic assumption that we can gain God's favor through good works. Divine grace and mercy are the beginning of our obedience and not its goal! Obedience to the law cannot accomplish salvation. As Paul noted, if there were a commandment that could give life, then justification would have come by the law (Galatians 3:21). Paul was clear that the law cannot justify or make us right with God (Galatians 2:21). For what the law could not do, because of the weakness of human flesh, God did by sending his Son to die on the cross (Romans 8:3).

The law, however, plays an important role within the divine embrace of the triune God who accepts and renews us by grace. The law is not a duty or drudgery but is something living and meaningful to life. The law is spiritual and essential to the delight of Christian living (Psalm 119:11, 15–16; Romans 7:14). We gladly have no other gods but God. We gladly give up all idols (Exodus 20:1–3). We make nothing absolute except God. Materialism, social influence, political agendas, social movements, or anything human, even things noble in themselves, can be made into destructive idols if granted the absolute significance that belongs alone to the triune God. True freedom only comes in service to God. Then, within the love of the Trinity's embrace, we can serve others freely by organizing and engaging in a number of strategies to proclaim the goodness of God and make the world a better place to live.

Trinitarian Hope

Our worship should grow richer, our witness stronger, and our participation more expansive in the liberating reign of God in all things. All of this takes place in the loving embrace of the triune God. But all of this also takes place towards God's liberating future for the world. This hope is one of those things we are most sure of.

I sat one evening with a small group of students in an introductory theology class. It was our final evening together, and we had just completed the lecture material for the course (an unusual occurrence!). We were engaged in a free-flowing question and answer session to pass the time creatively before our final session ended. I decided to take the opportunity to share with them those few ideas from the biblical message that had become most certain and foundational for me. The first was that God is the source of all things. I learned this from the heavenly Father. The second was that there is no place too dark or desperate for God, which is what I learned from the cross of Christ. The last was that there is real and enduring hope for the world, which is what I learned from the presence of the liberating Holy Spirit in the world, especially in the light of the Spirit's role in raising Jesus from the dead and in renewing all things after Christ's return. After most of the students finished writing these down, one looked up at me and said, "That will preach!" And indeed it does.

What does the embrace of the triune God offer the world in the future? We are all aware of the possible dangers that lurk in our future as a human race. Nuclear war, global warming, economic collapse, terrorism, and natural disasters all loom large on the horizon as possible threats to our happiness and survival. Seen from the natural eye, there seems to be no guarantee that history will end in anything but a nightmare. Even the Bible notes that there will be difficult days ahead due to the efforts of dark powers and evil intentions to take a last stand as history draws to an end. The book of Revelation speaks figuratively of four horsemen of these dark days that bring conquest, war, famine, and death as history draws to a close (Revelation 6). Is this what the future holds?

Not entirely. The book of Revelation also notes that God will remain on the throne during such days, weaving all of the affairs of history into a redemptive story in which the sacrificial love of Jesus and the Spirit of prophecy (who bears witness to the truth of Christ) fulfill their missions in the world in fulfillment of the Father's will. The darkest hours of human history will also be bright, for Revelation tells us that a countless throng of witnesses will emerge from these days as faithful witnesses to God's grace (Revelation 7:9–14). Moreover, the mere seven years of trial depicted at the end of time lead in Revelation to a towering thousand years of peace (see Revelation 20). Clearly, the message of the Bible is that where sin abounds, grace abounds much, much more (Romans 5:20).

The message of the Bible is that the triune God is leading all things towards the full healing effects of God's loving embrace. Within this embrace of the triune God, sin, sorrow, and death will be overthrown and the wounds inflicted by them healed. Notice what 1 Corinthians 15:22–28 states:

> For as in Adam all die, so in Christ all will be made

alive. But each in his own turn: Christ, the firstfruits; then, when he comes, those who belong to him. Then the end will come, when he hands over the kingdom to God the Father after he has destroyed all dominion, authority and power. For he must reign until he has put all his enemies under his feet. The last enemy to be destroyed is death. For he "has put everything under his feet." Now when it says that "everything" has been put under him, it is clear that this does not include God himself, who put everything under Christ. When he has done this, then the Son himself will be made subject to him who put everything under him, so that God may be all in all.

The goal as stated in the very first verse of the above text is that "all will be made alive" in Christ. God wishes that no one perish but that all come to repentance and eternal life (2 Peter 3:9). God hands over those who reject God's grace to their own darkness (Romans 1:24–28), but God also delivered up his very own Son to this same darkness so as to win back those who stray from God (Romans 4:25; 8:32). Indeed, God sent the one and only Son in the power of the Spirit not to condemn the world but to save it (John 3:16–17). What will the final fulfillment of salvation look like? What is the final hope for the world?

Our text quoted above tells us. The final enemy to be destroyed is death. At Jesus' resurrection, death was overcome. Death swallowed up Jesus at the cross but could not hold him. He burst it asunder at his resurrection. Death received a death blow but continued to have effects on the world. But the day will come in which all death and suffering will be eliminated. Notice what Revelation 21 states in this regard: "[God] will wipe every tear from their eyes. There will be no more death or mourning or crying or pain, for the old order of things has passed away" (Revelation 21:4).

This final victory over suffering and death will occur after Christ returns and the dead are raised. Then the final end will come in which all things are made new. The text from 1 Corinthians 15 above notes that something peculiar will happen at that time. First, the Father will submit all things to Christ. Then Christ will hand all things over to the Father. Last, God will be seen as "all in all." Let us unpack these points a bit.

First, the Father will submit all things to the Son. In conquering sin, suffering, and death in the Son through the power of the Holy Spirit, the Father will submit all things to the glory of the Son. The creation was made for the Son (Colossians 1:16) to be his household so that its inhabitants would recognize the Son as the head of all things, confessing him as Lord to the glory of the Father (Philippians 2:11). Next, the Son will hand all things over to the Father so that they will all glorify him. In other words, through the power of the Holy Spirit, the Father will use redeemed creation to bring glory to the Son and to lift him high, and the Son will then use the same redeemed creation to return glory to the Father.

How is the Spirit glorified? Precisely within the cloak of the redeemed creation, the Spirit is glorified in glorifying the Son and the Father. We are then glorified in our function in the hands of the triune God of glorifying God. Such glorifying will not be a prideful thing, for it is won through humble self-sacrifice. It will be rather a mutually uplifting expression of love and regard that will bring blessing too rich to imagine. The end of all things is that God is "all in all," the all-encompassing reality that pervades and glorifies all things.

This is a future that is worth looking forward to. It all takes place within the embrace of the triune God. The doctrine of the Trinity as developed through the logic of faith is not merely a piece of beautiful *wrship*

reasoning. It begins in love and adoration and will find its conclusion in the same. Those who neglect the biblical reasoning at the base of the Trinitarian doctrine have missed much. But those who think that the doctrine of the Trinity is only a logical puzzle have missed even more!

The doctrine of the Trinity seeks rather to call us all to recognize the rich variety and beauty of God's loving embrace. It seeks to show us how this embrace shapes our lives and our hopes. This Trinitarian embrace is the beginning and the end of all things related to life as God intended it. Rather than being an abstract intellectual puzzle, the doctrine of the Trinity is practical in the best sense of that term, for it shows us how God has embraced us and will embrace us ever more deeply as our lives and history itself draw to an end.

Study Questions:

1. Describe worship within the glory shared among the persons of the triune God.

2. Describe witness within the witness that is shared among the persons of the triune God.

3. Describe the ethics experienced within the reign or kingdom of the triune God.

4. Using 1 Corinthians 15:22–28, describe the final hope of history within the embrace of the triune God.